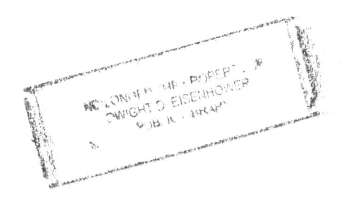

HOSPITAL LIABILITY LAW

Second Edition

by

Margaret C. Jasper

Oceana's Legal Almanac Series:
Law for the Layperson

Oceana®

NEW YORK

OXFORD

UNIVERSITY PRESS

Oxford University Press, Inc., publishes works that further Oxford University's objective of excellence in research, scholarship, and education.

Library of Congress Cataloging-in-Publication Data

Jasper, Margaret C.
  Hospital liability law / by Margaret C. Jasper. -- 2nd ed.
    p. cm. -- (Oceana's legal almanac series: law for the layperson)
  Includes bibliographical references.
  ISBN 978-0-19-533900-0 ((clothbound) : alk. paper)   1. Tort liability of hospitals--
United States--Popular works.   I. Title.
  KF3825.3.Z9J37 2008
  346.7303'1--dc22   2007048617

Note to Readers:
This publication is designed to provide accurate and authoritative information in regard to the subject matter covered. It is based upon sources believed to be accurate and reliable and is intended to be current as of the time it was written. It is sold with the understanding that the publisher is not engaged in rendering legal, accounting, or other professional services. If legal advice or other expert assistance is required, the services of a competent professional person should be sought. Also, to confirm that the information has not been affected or changed by recent developments, traditional legal research techniques should be used, including checking primary sources where appropriate.

(Based on the Declaration of Principles jointly adopted by a Committee of the American Bar Association and a Committee of Publishers and Associations.)

You may order this or any other Oxford University Press publication
by visiting the Oxford University Press website at www.oup.com

To My Husband Chris

Your love and support

are my motivation and inspiration

To My Sons, Michael, Nick and Chris

-and-

In memory of my son, Jimmy

Table of Contents

CHAPTER 6:
MEDICAL NEGLIGENCE LITIGATION

CHAPTER 7:
THE HIPAA PRIVACY RULE

APPENDICES

ABOUT THE AUTHOR

MARGARET C. JASPER is an attorney engaged in the general practice of law in South Salem, New York, concentrating in the areas of personal injury and entertainment law. Ms. Jasper holds a Juris Doctor degree from Pace University School of Law, White Plains, New York, is a member of the New York and Connecticut bars, and is certified to practice before the United States District Courts for the Southern and Eastern Districts of New York, the United States Court of Appeals for the Second Circuit, and the United States Supreme Court.

Ms. Jasper has been appointed to the law guardian panel for the Family Court of the State of New York, is a member of a number of professional organizations and associations, and is a New York State licensed real estate broker operating as Jasper Real Estate, in South Salem, New York.

Margaret Jasper maintains a website at http://www.JasperLawOffice.com.

In 2004, Ms. Jasper successfully argued a case before the New York Court of Appeals, which gives mothers of babies who are stillborn due to medical negligence the right to bring a legal action and recover emotional distress damages. This successful appeal overturned a 26-year old New York case precedent, which previously prevented mothers of stillborn babies from suing their negligent medical providers.

Ms. Jasper is the author and general editor of the following legal almanacs:

Adoption Law

AIDS Law

The Americans with Disabilities Act

Animal Rights Law

Auto Leasing

Bankruptcy Law for the Individual Debtor

Banks and their Customers

Becoming a Citizen

Buying and Selling Your Home

Commercial Law

Consumer Rights and the Law

Co-ops and Condominiums: Your Rights and Obligations As Owner

Copyright Law

Credit Cards and the Law

Custodial Rights

Dealing with Debt

Dictionary of Selected Legal Terms

Drunk Driving Law

DWI, DUI and the Law

Education Law

Elder Law

Employee Rights in the Workplace

Employment Discrimination Under Title VII

Environmental Law

Estate Planning

Everyday Legal Forms

Executors and Personal Representatives: Rights and Responsibilities

Guardianship and the Law

Harassment in the Workplace

Health Care and Your Rights

Health Care Directives

Hiring Household Help and Contractors: Your Rights and Obligations Under the Law

Home Mortgage Law Primer

Hospital Liability Law

How To Change Your Name

How To Form an LLC

How To Protect Your Challenged Child

How To Start Your Own Business

Identity Theft and How To Protect Yourself

Individual Bankruptcy and Restructuring

Injured on the Job: Employee Rights, Worker's Compensation and Disability Insurance Law

International Adoption

Juvenile Justice and Children's Law

Labor Law

Landlord-Tenant Law

Law for the Small Business Owner

The Law of Attachment and Garnishment

The Law of Buying and Selling

The Law of Capital Punishment

The Law of Child Custody

The Law of Contracts

The Law of Debt Collection

The Law of Dispute Resolution

The Law of Immigration

The Law of Libel and Slander

The Law of Medical Malpractice

The Law of No-Fault Insurance

The Law of Obscenity and Pornography

The Law of Personal Injury

The Law of Premises Liability

The Law of Product Liability

The Law of Speech and the First Amendment

Lemon Laws

Living Together: Practical Legal Issues

Marriage and Divorce

Missing and Exploited Children: How to Protect Your Child

Motor Vehicle Law

Nursing Home Negligence

Patent Law

Pet Law

Prescription Drugs

Privacy and the Internet: Your Rights and Expectations Under the Law

Probate Law

Protecting Your Business: Disaster Preparation and the Law

Real Estate Law for the Homeowner and Broker

Religion and the Law

Retirement Planning

The Right to Die

Rights of Single Parents

Small Claims Court

Social Security Law

Special Education Law

Teenagers and Substance Abuse

Trademark Law

Trouble Next Door: What to do With Your Neighbor

Victim's Rights Law

Violence Against Women

Welfare: Your Rights and the Law

What if It Happened to You: Violent Crimes and Victims' Rights

What if the Product Doesn't Work: Warranties & Guarantees

Workers' Compensation Law

Your Child's Legal Rights: An Overview

Your Rights in a Class Action Suit

Your Rights as a Tenant

Your Rights Under the Family and Medical Leave Act

You've Been Fired: Your Rights and Remedies

INTRODUCTION

This legal Almanac explores the area of law known generally as "hospital liability." Historically, hospitals enjoyed limited liability under malpractice law insofar as they were not liable for the acts of the physicians who used their facilities to treat patients.

Over the years, this area of law has evolved, and hospitals have been subject to malpractice actions for their own independent negligence as well as the negligence of staff physicians, residents, interns, nurses, and other hospital health care providers and employees under the theory of *respondeat superior*. In addition, in jurisdictions that subscribe to the corporate negligence doctrine, hospitals may also be liable for the negligence of attending private physicians, for example, if they failed to properly investigate their credentials before granting them privileges to practice in the hospital.

Hospitals are now routinely named as defendants in medical malpractice actions under a variety of theories of liability. In general, medical malpractice involves the commission of a tort—a wrongful act—as do all personal injury actions. A medical malpractice action generally carries a shortened statute of limitations, a limit on damage awards and a cap on legal fees. In addition, many states require that a physician find that the case has some merit before it can be filed.

Negligence is the predominant theory of medical malpractice litigation. Other theories of liability include lack of informed consent and/or informed refusal; unauthorized treatment that may lead to a cause of action for battery; breach of privacy for the unauthorized release of a patient's medical record; and breach of contract. Responsible parties may include physicians, residents, interns, nurses, hospitals, mental health professionals, anesthesiologists, and other persons who provide medical care.

This Almanac sets forth the duties and responsibilities a hospital owes to its patients, and its liability for breaching those duties. In addition, the elements necessary to prove the various theories of liability that support a *prima facie* medical negligence claim, the defenses to such claims, the litigation procedures unique to medical malpractice, the responsible parties and apportionment of liability, and the damages recoverable are also discussed.

This Almanac also discusses the topic of health care directives and the patient's right to participate in their own health care decisions. A living will and a durable power of attorney for health care are examples of important health care directives. The patient's right to refuse medical treatment is examined, including advance medical directives, health care proxies, do not resuscitate orders, and the patient's right to pain management. Legal issues concerning a medical provider's failure to carry out a patient's wishes are also discussed. Additional topics include religious objections to executing a living will, capacity issues such as age and mental competence, and informed consent.

In addition, this Almanac explores the problem of nursing home negligence and abuse, the types of neglect and abuse, and the ways to recognize and address these problems. The legislation developed to prevent nursing home neglect and abuse is also discussed, including the legal rights of the nursing home resident, and the remedies available under the law.

Readers are cautioned, however, when researching a particular problem, not to rely on a general discussion of the law, but to always check the law of their own jurisdictions.

The Appendices provide sample documents, applicable statutes, resource directories, medical terminology and other pertinent information and data. The Glossary contains definitions of many of the terms used throughout the Almanac.

CHAPTER 1:
HOSPITAL ORGANIZATION

IN GENERAL

Hospitals are corporations that are generally organized as either public or private entities. A public hospital is created by the act of a governmental authority and controlled under the auspices of that government unit by the governing body of the hospital. A private hospital is either (i) voluntary—i.e., a charitable not-for-profit corporation; (ii) investor-owned—operating for profit on behalf of shareholders; or a (iii) member of a multi-unit system which consists of multiple facilities sharing management and services under a single ownership.

A directory of state licensing agencies for medical facilities is set forth in Appendix 1.

THE JOINT COMMISSION

The Joint Commission, formerly known as the Joint Commission on Accreditation of Healthcare Organizations, is an independent, not-for-profit organization governed by a 29-member Board of Commissioners that includes physicians, administrators, nurses, employers, a labor representative, health plan leaders, quality experts, ethicists, a consumer advocate and educators. The Joint Commission's stated mission is to improve the safety and quality of care provided to the public through the provision of health care accreditation and related services that support performance improvement in health care organizations.

To carry out its mission, the Joint Commission evaluates and accredits more than 15,000 health care organizations and programs in the United States, and promulgates state-of-the-art standards that focus on improving the quality and safety of care provided by health care organizations. Joint Commission standards address the organization's level of performance in key functional areas, such as patient rights, patient treatment, and infection control. The standards focus not simply on an organization's ability to provide safe, high quality care, but on its actual performance as well.

The Joint Commission's comprehensive accreditation process evaluates an organization's compliance with these standards and other accreditation requirements. Joint Commission accreditation is recognized nationwide as a symbol of quality that reflects an organization's commitment to meeting certain performance standards. To earn and maintain The Joint Commission's Gold Seal of Approval, an organization must undergo an on-site survey by a Joint Commission survey team at least every three years.

THE GOVERNING BODY

The governing body of a public hospital generally consists of individuals who are publicly elected or appointed by an elected official. Members of the governing body of a private hospital are elected by shareholders. The governing board is responsible for appointing a chief executive officer who manages the daily operation of the hospital, and implements the policies set by the board.

According to the Joint Commission, the governing body of a hospital is responsible for its operation, including establishing policy; maintaining quality patient care; and institutional management and planning. In addition, the governing body has the ultimate responsibility and authority for appointment and oversight of the organization's medical staff.

For example, the governing body delegates the responsibility of making recommendations concerning medical staff appointments, reappointments, revocations, and the delineation of clinical privileges, to the medical staff. The courts have repeatedly upheld the hospital's legal duty to ensure competency of individual medical staff members.

In order to maintain accreditation with the Joint Commission, the governing body must adopt bylaws. The bylaws must contain an organizational chart and specify the role and purpose of the hospital. Many hospitals form committees to which responsibilities are delegated, which may include (i) an executive committee; (ii) a joint conference committee; and (iii) an institutional planning committee.

MEDICAL STAFF

To comply with Joint Commission regulations, the medical staff of a hospital must consist of fully-licensed physicians, and may also include other non-physician licensed individuals, such as dentists, podiatrists and nurse practitioners. The medical staff establishes its own bylaws that must be approved by the governing body, and must set forth an organizational chart that delineates lines of responsibility and accountability.

The medical staff is responsible for overseeing patient care as well as the professional conduct of its members. The medical staff is also responsible for approving or denying staff privileges to medical personnel, a responsibility delegated to it by the governing body. Nevertheless, the governing body still maintains ultimate authority to approve or deny such appointments.

Hospital Privileges

When a doctor is granted privileges at a particular hospital, this means he or she has permission to work in the hospital. For example, a doctor with privileges is allowed to admit patients to the hospital, perform procedures, and order treatment, testing, and medication, etc. If a doctor does not have privileges at the hospital where his or her patient wants to be admitted, the doctor must advise the patient that he or she must be treated at the hospital where the doctor has privileges or, in the alternative, refer the patient to a doctor who has privileges at the desired hospital.

An applicant for hospital privileges must meet certain minimum professional criteria relating to their education, experience, competence, licensure and health. This is known as "credentialing"—i.e., assuring professional competency. Credentialing is an important part of the hospital application process. Credentialing demonstrates that the doctor is qualified to perform the procedures he or she has requested. Credentialing usually requires documentation of proof of graduation, state licenses, diagnostic and therapeutic certification, malpractice insurance, completion of continuing education requirements, professional experience, curriculum vitae, and other similar documentation.

Joint Commission Recommendations

The Joint Commission has issued recommendations that a hospital should follow in verifying the qualifications of a physician applicant. According to these recommendations, the hospital medical staff member responsible for verifying physician qualifications should ascertain:

    1. Evidence of current licensure;

2. Relevant training and/or experience;

3. Health status;

4. The ability of the hospital to provide adequate facilities and supportive services for the applicant and his or her patients;

5. Patient care needs for additional staff members with the applicant's skill and training;

6. Current evidence of adequate professional liability insurance;

7. The geographic location of the applicant;

8. Involvement in any professional liability action;

9. Previously successful or currently pending challenges to any licensure or registration;

10. Loss of medical staff membership or clinical privileges at another hospital; and

11. Peer recommendations.

In addition to the Joint Commission recommendations, federal law requires a hospital to report any peer review action, or surrender of clinical privileges concerning a staff physician, to the Department of Health and Human Services (DHHS). When a physician applies for privileges or renewal of privileges, a hospital is required to request those reports from DHHS and, if they fail to do so, this would create a presumption that the hospital had knowledge of the reported information concerning that physician.

Denial of Privileges

Grounds for denial of an application for professional privileges may include:

1. The type of education and degree obtained by the applicant, e.g., chiropractors are generally excluded;

2. Inadequate professional liability insurance;

3. Behavior and personal conduct; and

4. The needs of the hospital and its patients.

In addition, if an applicant has been involved in medical negligence litigation, loss of license, or loss of privileges at another hospital, his or her application for privileges will be carefully scrutinized and may be denied.

A hospital that fails to make reasonable inquiries into the background of an applicant may ultimately be found responsible under the corporate negligence doctrine for negligent supervision or retention if it employs or grants privileges to an incompetent physician.

A directory of state physician licensing bureaus is set forth in Appendix 2.

THE NURSING STAFF

The Joint Commission standards require hospitals to establish a nursing department, headed by a registered nurse administrator, who ideally has earned a baccalaureate degree in nursing. The nursing department is responsible for establishing standards of nursing care; approving the employment qualifications for its nurses; and conducting evaluations of the staff. The nursing department is also required to set forth an organizational plan delineating lines of responsibility and accountability.

It is the responsibility of a hospital to make sure that a sufficient number of registered nurses are on duty at all times to maintain quality patient care. Hospitals may be held liable for damages resulting from a nursing staff shortage.

In considering whether there are a sufficient number of nurses on duty, certain factors will be evaluated, including the number of patients in the unit and the level of care they require; the degree of on-duty staff expertise; the availability of support personnel; and the geographic makeup of the unit.

CHAPTER 2:
PROTECTING YOURSELF FROM
MEDICAL MISTAKES

IN GENERAL

Unfortunately, recent statistics demonstrate that between 44,000 and 88,000 hospital patients die each year as a result of medical negligence. Further, this figure does not include malpractice-related deaths that occur outside the hospital setting.

The Association for Responsible Medicine (ARM), an entity concerned with preventing and exposing medical negligence, has gathered some startling statistics about medical negligence:

1. Over one million hospital patients will suffer an injury as the result of a medical mistake.

2. More than 180,000 die partly as the result of a medical mistake according to the Harvard Medical Practice Study.

3. No government agency—state or Federal—maintains a record of this epidemic.

4. Studies show that medical malpractice is more likely if a doctor has made mistakes in the past.

5. Doctors with many malpractice settlements are allowed to retain their licenses and hospital privileges.

6. Doctors are not required to carry liability insurance to cover patients injured by a medical mistake.

7. Doctors may perform surgery that was not authorized because of medical consent laws that protect doctors.

8. A doctor may allow another person to perform surgery without the patient's consent.

9. At some hospitals, 18% to 36% of patients may suffer from a medical mistake that causes injury or death.

10. Medical mistakes usually go unreported.

11. State laws generally prohibit the release of a hospital report on a medical mistake even to the injured patient or his/her family.

RESEARCH THE HOSPITAL'S CREDENTIALS

In General

Hospitalization is a serious matter. However, all to often, prospective patients do not look into the background of the hospital they are preparing to enter. It is critical, in order to be protected from medical mistakes, that the patient investigate the hospital that will be responsible for his or her care while undergoing a medical procedure. There is much information readily available to the individual who requests it.

For example, hospitals are required by law to maintain a statistical record on all procedures. The prospective patient can request this information. Also, he or she may inquire about the credentials of the hospital's staff, including their nurses and others associated with the prospective patient's daily care.

The prospective patient should familiarize themselves with the hospital's "Patient Bill of Rights," which lists the patient's rights in reference to many aspects of care, such as confidentiality, safety, access to care, communications, hospital rules and regulations.

Joint Commission Recommendations

As discussed in Chapter 1, "Hospital Organization,"the Joint Commission is the nation's predominant standards-setting and accrediting body in health care, and evaluates and accredits thousands of health care organizations and programs in the United States. The Joint Commission recommends the following five steps to obtaining safer health care.

Step One: Ask Questions

The patient is advised to speak freely with their medical provider if they have any concerns. It is okay to ask questions and to expect answers you can understand. Thus, it is important to choose a doctor whom you feel comfortable talking to about your health and treatment. In addition, it is advisable to take a relative or friend with you if this will assist you in asking questions and understanding the answers.

Step Two: Investigate Prescription Medications

It is important to keep a list of all medicines you take and to advise both your medical providers and pharmacist about all the medicines you take, including over-the-counter medicines such as aspirin, ibuprofen, vitamins and herbals. You should also advise your medical providers and pharmacist about any drug allergies you may have.

When you are given a prescription, ask the pharmacist about side effects and what foods or other things to avoid while taking the medication. Be sure to read the label, including warnings, and make sure you know how to properly administer the medication. Make sure the medication you receive is the medication your doctor ordered for you. If the medication looks different than you expected, ask the pharmacist about the difference, if any.

Step Three: Obtain Test Results

Make sure you get the results of all tests and procedures performed. If you have any questions, ask the doctor or nurse when and how you will obtain the results. Further, don't assume the results are fine if you don't get them when expected. Follow up and call the doctor. If you have any questions about what the test results mean, ask for an explanation.

Step Four: Choose a Hospital

If you need hospital care, talk with your doctor about your care options. You should verify which hospitals are accepted by your insurance, HMO or PPO plan. If you have more than one hospital to choose from, ask the doctor which hospital has the best care for your condition and ask him or her to explain the advantages or special characteristics of each hospital where he or she practices.

Hospitals do a good job of treating a wide range of problems. For some procedures, however, such as heart bypass surgery, research shows results are often better at hospitals doing a lot of these procedures.

You can also research your local hospital by consulting the Joint Commission's "Quality Check" publication on the internet. "Quality Check" is a comprehensive internet guide to accredited organizations, where a consumer can search for quality information on their local hospital.

Some of the questions and concerns the Joint Commission recommends a patient inquire about before choosing a hospital include:

1. Is the hospital conveniently located? Can you and your family get there easily for scheduled as well as emergency medical care?

2. Is the hospital accredited by a nationally recognized accrediting body, such as the Joint Commission?

3. Does the hospital have a written description of its services and fees and what resources, if any the hospital provides to help you find financial assistance if you need it?

4. Is the hospital clean? Visit the hospital and look around. Ask to see the waiting rooms and patient care rooms. Does the waiting room look comfortable? Would you want to recuperate in the patient rooms? Do the patient rooms have comfortable chairs for visitors? Do you have privacy in the room?

5. Do the services and specialties provided by the hospital meet your specific medical needs? Do you have a medical condition requiring specialized attention?

6. What is the hospital's success record in carrying out the specific medical procedure you need and how often is the particular procedure done?

7. What is the specific training of the physician who will perform the procedure?

8. Ask to see a copy of the hospital's patient rights and responsibilities information.

9. Who will be responsible for maintaining your personal care plan and how will you and/or your family be kept up-to-date on your medical care?

10. Does the hospital have social workers and what services do the social workers provide? For example, social workers usually help patients and their families find emotional, social, clinical, physical and financial support services.

11. Will a discharge plan be developed for you before you leave the hospital and will the hospital provide you with the necessary training to continue your care in your home after you have been discharged?

Step Five: Ask About the Surgery

Make sure you understand what will happen if you need surgery. You, your doctor and surgeon should all agree on exactly what will be done during the operation. Ask how long the surgery will take, what will happen after the surgery and how you will feel during your recovery.

In addition, ask who will be in charge of your care while you are in the hospital. Advise the surgeon, anesthesiologist and nurses if you have allergies or have ever had a bad reaction to anesthesia. Before you leave the hospital, ask about follow-up care and understand all instructions.

Obtain a Second Opinion

When faced with the decision about whether to submit to a particular medical procedure or treatment, it is wise for the patient to obtain a second opinion from a physician not affiliated with the primary physician. It is also important to make sure that the intended procedure is FDA-approved. Surgeries without FDA approval are considered experimental and results therefore are uncertain.

Preparing for an Emergency

The information above is designed to assist the prospective patient in investigating a hospital in anticipation of a planned medical procedure or treatment. However, an individual may find that he or she is in the midst of an unexpected health crisis requiring the emergency admission to a hospital. There are ways to prepare oneself for such an unanticipated event, as set forth below.

Keep a Medical Journal

Every individual should keep a medical journal that sets forth important health-related information, such as:

1. Any allergies they have to medications or foods and the anticipated reaction;

2. An outline of past hospitalizations, surgeries and significant medical conditions and treatments;

3. Current medical problems, if any;

4. A list of prescription drugs being taken along with the instructions concerning dosage;

5. A list of over-the-counter medications being taken along with information on the purpose and frequency of the medications being taken;

6. Periodic height, weight and blood pressure measurements;

7. Insurance information; and

8. Any other information related to the individual's health.

Execute Advance Directives

In addition to keeping a detailed medical journal, one should execute advanced directives and a durable power of attorney for health care, and provide copies of these documents to their health care provider, attorney, and family members. Advanced directives are discussed more fully in Chapter 5, "Advance Health Care Directives."

RESEARCH THE PHYSICIAN'S CREDENTIALS

The American Medical Association provides background and credentialing information on physicians at its website [http://www.ama-assn.org]. You can find out where your prospective doctor went to medical school, whether they are board-certified, as well as their office address and phone number.

The American Board of Medical Specialties operates a website [http://www.abms.org/] where you can find out if a specific physician has been certified as a specialist by one of their specialty boards.

In addition, the Federation of State Medical Boards operates a website [http://www.fsmb.org] which has direct links to all of the state medical licensing boards. You can access your state's medical board to find out the status of a doctor's license and whether he or she has ever been the subject of disciplinary procedures. Several states now also include medical malpractice and hospital disciplinary action information on their own websites.

The County Clerk in a particular jurisdiction generally provides public access to its database of legal actions filed in the jurisdiction. It is possible to research whether a particular doctor has been the subject of any lawsuits, and even review copies of the litigation papers, such as the actual complaint, which are on file with the Clerk's office.

There are also companies who specialize in checking the background of health care providers. Health Care Choices is a New York not-for-profit corporation dedicated to educating the public about the nation's health care system. HealthGrades.com, Inc. is a private company that provides "report cards" on doctors, hospitals, health plans and nursing homes

CHAPTER 3:
THEORIES OF LIABILITY

THE HOSPITAL'S DUTY TO TREAT

Under the common law, an individual was not generally obligated to prevent an injury to another, absent special circumstances. This common law doctrine includes the right of a hospital to refuse to admit or treat a person who comes in seeking admission or treatment.

The courts have generally deferred to the medical judgment of hospital personnel, and refused to require hospitals to use their medical resources for every person seeking treatment. Nevertheless, as further discussed below, there are circumstances under which the Courts have held that the common law doctrine of no duty to admit or treat does not apply.

Emergency Situations

Hospitals are generally required to treat seriously injured or sick persons on an emergency basis, and their refusal to treat such people has resulted in the imposition of liability. However, the nature of an emergency is subjective and it is not always apparent whether a patient's condition actually constitutes an emergency.

In general, emergencies involve events that are sudden or unforeseen. However, even where an individual's condition is not in an emergency status at the time they arrive at the hospital, requiring that person to seek medical attention elsewhere may turn a non-emergency situation into an emergency. Thus, a hospital may also be required to prevent the occurrence of an emergency.

For example, if a woman is pregnant and in the early stages of labor, her status would not be considered an emergency. However, if requiring the woman to seek alternative medical treatment would mean that she would have to travel a very long distance, the receiving hospital may be required to treat the woman regardless of her present status.

Discrimination

Many federal and state statutes prohibit unreasonable discrimination by hospitals in their refusal to admit or treat, despite the common law doctrine.

Discrimination on the Basis of Race, Color, Religion or National Origin

Hospitals are constitutionally prohibited from refusing to treat or admit a particular person due to their race, color, religion or national origin.

Discrimination on the Basis of Inability to Pay

In addition, hospitals are not permitted to discriminate against patients based on their inability to pay for their treatment, particularly where the hospital receives federal assistance. Under the Hill-Burton Act, 42 U.S.C. §291-2910, which established funding for construction and modernization of hospitals, a 20-year obligation was placed upon hospitals that received federal funds to provide free care and community service to indigent patients. In addition, many states have enacted legislation prohibiting hospitals from discriminating against individuals based on their ability to pay.

The Emergency Treatment and Active Labor Act (EMTALA)

Under the Emergency Treatment and Active Labor Act of 1986 (EMTALA)—also known as the "Anti-Dumping Act"—Medicare provider hospitals are prohibited from transferring, discharging or refusing to treat a patient solely because of his or her inability to pay for treatment where the hospital has the resources to provide the needed care. Hospitals that violate EMTALA are subject to civil liabilities, including monetary sanctions.

Under the EMTALA, the hospital must provide an appropriate medical screening examination to any person seeking treatment or admission at an emergency department, to determine whether an emergency exists. If the individual refuses to submit to the medical examination, the hospital will have been deemed to have complied with the Act, provided it adequately informs the individual of the risks associated with his or her refusal to be examined.

As defined by the Act, an emergency exists if the individual's medical condition could reasonably be expected to put the individual's health in serious jeopardy, or result in a serious impairment to bodily functions, or serious dysfunction of any bodily organ or part.

The Act also applies to pregnant women having contractions if there is not enough time to safely transfer the woman to another hospital before delivery without posing a threat to her health or safety, or the health and safety of her unborn child.

If the medical screening examination determines that the individual has an emergency medical condition, they may not be transferred or discharged unless their medical condition is stabilized.

An exception to the rule exists if the patient requests a transfer, in writing, after being thoroughly advised of the risks of the transfer and the hospital's obligation to treat the patient. In addition, another exception exists if a physician certifies that the medical benefits of the transfer outweigh the risks.

Child Abuse and Rape Victims

Federal and state regulations generally require hospitals to treat children who have been abused or raped. In addition, hospitals are also required to notify state child protective agencies when there is suspicion of child abuse under mandatory reporting statutes. Most jurisdictions provide a hospital with criminal and civil immunity from lawsuits brought as a result of reporting abuse, provided the hospital makes the report in good faith. Therefore, it is incumbent upon the hospital to make a detailed record of its reasons for making a report. Inadequate notes may cancel the immunity and subject the hospital to liability.

INFORMED CONSENT

An individual has an absolute right to prevent an unauthorized contact with his or her person. In medical malpractice litigation, treatment without the patient's consent may be actionable as battery. Prior to performing any type of invasive procedure or non-customary treatment, the health care provider is obligated to obtain the patient's informed consent.

If the health care provider does not obtain such consent, any treatment rendered is deemed unauthorized and the health care provider will be liable to the patient for any negative consequences.

A patient gives consent to medical treatment either by (1) express consent or (2) implied consent.

Express Consent

Express consent is obtained either in writing or orally. The health care provider is required to fully disclose all of the known and significant facts relevant to the procedure, in layperson's language, so that the patient can make an intelligent decision as to whether to go forward with the treatment.

The following information should be provided to the patient to satisfy the informed consent requirement:

1. The diagnosis of the patient's condition and the prognosis without the proposed treatment;

2. The nature of the proposed treatment;

3. The goal to be achieved by the proposed treatment and the chance that the treatment will be successful;

4. The risks of the proposed treatment;

5. Any alternative treatments to the proposed treatment;

6. Identify:

(a) The health care provider(s) who discussed the proposed treatment with the patient;

(b) The health care provider(s) who will perform the proposed treatment;

7. Obtain consent to deviate from the proposed treatment in case of unforeseen circumstances;

8. Obtain consent to dispose of any tissue, organs or other body parts, if needed, for pathological study or research;

9. Acknowledgement that the patient's questions were fully discussed and adequately answered;

10. The patient's and/or legal guardian's signature, the signature of a witness, and the date, time, and location that the consent form was signed. If the patient is a minor, the parents may consent to the procedure, or, in the case of divorce, it is usually the parent having legal custody who may consent.

For people with special needs, such as a hearing or vision disability, or the inability to understand English, medical facilities must make skilled interpreters available to patients to explain and answer questions about their rights and provide information on how they can protect those rights. Translations and/or transcriptions of important forms, instructions and information must be provided if the patient requires them for an understanding of the documents.

Where the health care provider has failed to obtain such consent, or where the quality of the consent is challenged, the patient may claim lack of informed consent for the procedure.

A sample Informed Consent Agreement is set forth in Appendix 3.

Implied Consent

Implied consent is obtained, for example, when a patient submits to a *simple* procedure. However, there is no implied consent where the procedure is invasive or non-customary.

Further, once a surgeon begins an internal surgical procedure, there is a presumption of implied consent if the surgeon does other *necessary* procedures in the process. This is so even if there are relatives in the vicinity because the surgeon is not permitted to leave the operating room, once the surgery has begun, to obtain consent.

However, such implied consent only applies to necessary procedures. If the procedure is elective, the surgeon has the duty to delay until he receives the necessary consent for the additional surgery.

Implied consent also applies in emergency situations. If the emergency involves risk to the patient's life, or the patient is unable to give consent due to unconsciousness, coma or other incompetence, it has been held that the patient would have consented to the treatment if he or she were able, thus consent is implied in such situations.

The existence of the emergency should be entered into the medical records, including the reason why the procedure was necessary, e.g., the patient's airway was blocked and an emergency tracheotomy was necessary or the patient would have choked to death.

Lack of Informed Consent

Lack of informed consent means that the patient did not fully understand what the health care provider was going to do, and was injured as a result of the health care provider's action. Further, the patient claims that if he had known what the health care provider planned to do, the patient would not have consented and, therefore, would have avoided the injury.

Absent an emergency, if the health care provider is able to ascertain, in advance of a surgical procedure, all of the possible alternatives available if an unexpected situation should arise during the operation, the patient should be informed of the alternatives and given the chance to decide if those alternatives are acceptable before the health care provider proceeds with the procedure.

Informed Consent and Prescription Drugs

More often than not, a patient is prescribed medication without any details given to them about the particular medication. They simply take the often illegibly handwritten prescription to the pharmacy, have it filled, and start taking the drug according to the label's directions.

However, patients have the right to know much more about the medicines that they are taking, and should take advantage of those rights.

Most problems associated with prescription drugs occur because the patient did not receive enough information concerning the medicine to use it properly. For example, they are unaware of what side effects to expect, or they improperly mix the medication with a food or drink, or another medication. The improper use of prescription medications can be deadly.

It is important to ask your medical provider every question you may have concerning a medication that is prescribed for you. A patient has the right to be informed about all aspects of their medical treatment, including the risks and benefits of the medicines prescribed; the potential side effects; and the necessity of monitoring the medication's effects. The patient also has the right to know the results of any tests that demonstrate whether or not the medication is working. For example, if the medical provider prescribes a cholesterol-reducing drug, the patient should be advised whether or not the medication is effectively reducing their cholesterol level.

The patient should also discuss with their medical provider all of the medicines that they are presently taking, including over-the-counter medicines, and whether there are any concerns about the interaction between those medicines with the medicine being prescribed. In particular, a patient has the right to the following information:

1. The name of the medicine and how it is intended to treat the patient's condition;

2. The dosage, frequency and duration prescribed, and whether there are refills available;

3. The foods, drinks, and other medicines that may negatively interact with the medication being prescribed;

4. The potential side effects of the medicine, and instructions on how to proceed should the patient experience those side effects;

5. An explanation of any terms or directions the patient does not understand.

6. A copy of any written information that may be available concerning the medication they are being prescribed.

The Food and Drug Administration (FDA) provides updated information about medication errors, including specific drugs that have been confused with one another. The information has been compiled based on voluntary reports received from consumers, doctors and other clinicians, as well as mandatory reports from manufacturers. Information concerning medication errors is available from the FDA on-line at www.fda.gov.

Informed Consent and the Responsibilities of Health Care Providers

In order to ensure a patient has been adequately provided with information sufficient to make an informed decision, health care providers should:

1. Provide patients with easily understood information and opportunity to decide among treatment options consistent with the informed consent process.

2. Discuss all treatment options with a patient in a culturally competent manner, including the option of no treatment at all.

3. Ensure that persons with disabilities have effective communications with members of the health system in making health care decisions.

4. Discuss all current treatments a patient may be undergoing, including those alternative treatments that are self-administered.

5. Discuss all risks, benefits, and consequences of treatment or nontreatment.

6. Give patients the opportunity to refuse treatment and to express preferences about future treatment decisions.

7. Discuss the use of advance directives—both living wills and durable powers of attorney for health care—with patients and their designated family members.

8. Abide by the decisions made by the patient and/or the patient's designated representative consistent with the informed consent process.

A table of risks associated with common medical procedures is set forth in Appendix 4.

NEGLIGENT HOSPITAL DISCHARGE

A patient is generally approved for discharge from a hospital based on the medical opinion of his or her attending physician. Thus, a hospital would not be liable for the attending physician's decision to discharge unless the corporate negligence doctrine discussed below applies to the situation.

However, when a patient has been under the care and treatment of hospital personnel, the decision to discharge must be carefully considered and medically sound. It would be a departure from the required standard of care to prematurely release a patient who has been admitted or treated without a proper medical analysis.

A court will carefully scrutinize the hospital's reasons for discharging a patient, particularly where it appears that the discharge may have been motivated by the patient's inability to pay for treatment.

Diagnostic Testing

Prior to discharge, the treating physician must order the performance of all appropriate diagnostic tests, such as CT scans, x-rays, blood tests, etc. In addition, the results of those tests should be discussed with the patient prior to discharge.

A hospital may be liable for prematurely discharging a patient prior to performing the tests and relating the results if the patient subsequently suffers harm from the early release.

Discharge Clearance

In general, to avoid liability, a hospital should have a licensed physician review the patient's chart and perform a physical examination prior to discharge in order to "clear" the discharge. In addition, hospital personnel should properly instruct the patient regarding such matters as diet, limits on activities, medication, at-home treatment, etc. Ideally such instructions should be in writing. Further, the discharge instructions should be documented in the patient's medical chart.

Discharge Against Medical Advice

If a patient seeks discharge from the hospital against the medical advice of the treating physician, it is important that the patient be thoroughly advised of the risks associated with premature discharge. This is generally known as "informed refusal" to treatment, and should be carefully documented in the patient's medical chart should the patient suffer injuries as a result of their decision.

In addition, the patient should be required to sign a release form absolving hospital personnel from any injuries caused by the release against medical advice.

LIABILITY FOR MISCELLANEOUS HOSPITAL SERVICES

There are a number of miscellaneous hospital services that commonly give rise to litigation. Some of the more common issues are discussed below.

Blood Transfusions

In general, courts have refused to apply a product liability standard to the use of contaminated blood by a hospital in the treatment of its patients. Thus, hospital patients who receive a tainted blood transfusion may not recover under the theories of breach of warranty or strict liability against the hospital. The courts have generally held that furnishing blood is incidental and secondary to hospital services, and cannot be considered a "sale" under a product liability theory of recovery.

In addition, some courts have also recognized the inherent difficulty in screening blood for the existence of certain impurities, such as the hepatitis virus. Thus, blood has basically been deemed an "unavoidably unsafe product," the use of which cannot be prohibited due to society's critical need for the product. Therefore, it would be unfair and dangerous to impose a strict liability standard upon the medical profession, and would only make health care providers fearful of using blood products until such time as a foolproof test is devised.

Nevertheless, a hospital is liable for its own negligence in supplying tainted blood. Thus, if a hospital knew, or should have known, that blood was contaminated, and, nonetheless, used the blood in a transfusion, the hospital would be liable for breaching its duty to the patient.

Although a hospital is not under a duty to retest blood it receives from a blood bank, it is responsible for testing blood obtained directly from donors.

Organ Transplants

In connection with organ transplants, a hospital owes a duty to the donee to take reasonable care in the selection of an organ donor, and in the subsequent handling of the organ following donation.

Medication Administration

A hospital may be held liable for the negligence of its employees in administering medication to its patients. For example, an attending private physician routinely leaves instructions concerning the administration of medication with the nursing staff. The nursing staff is responsible for carrying out the physician's instructions in the proper administration of the drug.

Thus, the hospital may be liable to the patient if the nursing staff improperly administers the drug, e.g., if they delay administering the drug; fail to administer the drug; administer the wrong drug or an incorrect dosage of the drug; or fail to monitor the patient following administration of the drug.

In addition, if the physician's medication instructions are incorrect or improper, the hospital may also be liable if its employees nevertheless follow the improper orders where knowledge of the mistake is properly imputed to the staff, e.g., they knew or should have known that the instructions were wrong.

Anesthesia Administration

A hospital is vicariously liable for the negligence of the anesthesiologists it employs under the theory of *respondeat superior*. In addition, a hospital would also be responsible for the negligence of an incompetent anesthesiologist who works as an independent contractor, provided the jurisdiction subscribes to the corporate negligence doctrine. To recover, the plaintiff must demonstrate that the hospital knew, or should have known that the anesthesiologist was incompetent.

Although the administration of anesthesia is commonly performed, it is nonetheless a complex process with inherent risks and hazards. A patient should be thoroughly informed of all of the attendant risks of anesthesia, and any available alternatives. A hospital is required to have an anesthesiologist available for its patients at all times.

Surgical Procedures

A hospital is responsible for negligence that occurs in the operating room if the actions were those of hospital employees. A hospital may also be deemed liable for failing to adequately supervise its employees in the performance of surgical procedures. Again, the theory of liability is *respondeat superior*.

Nevertheless, a private attending surgeon is considered responsible for everything that occurs in the operating room, including the hospital personnel working with him in carrying out the surgical procedure. This is known as the "captain of the ship" doctrine.

Under this doctrine, the surgeon would also be vicariously liable for all of the personnel in the operating room, including hospital employees such as residents, interns and nurses. However, if the hospital employees are negligent in carrying out the surgeon's instructions, the hospital would be liable for their negligence.

Pathology Department

A surgical procedure often follows an examination of biopsied tissue by the hospital's pathology department. If an attending private surgeon relies on the accuracy of an employee pathologist's diagnosis of the tissue sample, the hospital may be held liable for any injuries resulting from that diagnosis.

For example, if the employee pathologist incorrectly diagnoses a skin tissue sample as a malignant melanoma, and the attending private surgeon acts upon that diagnosis by making a large incision in a patient's back, causing extensive scarring, the hospital may be responsible if the employee pathologist's diagnosis of malignancy turns out to be incorrect. The patient in such a case would have suffered unnecessary pain, suffering and permanent scarring.

Autopsies

In general, the performance of an autopsy requires consent by the surviving spouse or next of kin, absent some statutory authorization for the autopsy. If a hospital performs an autopsy without proper authorization, it may be liable.

Anatomical Donations

If a decedent signed some type of writing authorizing a donation of his or her organs under the Uniform Anatomical Gift Act, this writing authorizes the donation. Nevertheless, some states have held that hospital administrators must still advise a decedent's next of kin of their right to arrange for donation of the anatomical gift.

If there is no writing evidencing a desire to make an anatomical donation, permission must first be obtained from the next of kin prior to removing a decedent's bodily organ.

A donor's statement regarding anatomical gifts is set forth in Appendix 5.

MEDICAL NEGLIGENCE

Negligence is the predominant theory of medical malpractice litigation. As discussed in Chapter 6, "Medical Negligence Litigation," liability for medical negligence cannot exist unless there is a health care provider/patient relationship that creates a duty on the part of the health care provider to render acceptable medical care to the patient.

In the case of a hospital, this would occur when the patient visits the hospital and receives treatment by a hospital employee or other health care provider for whom the hospital is found to be responsible. Hospitals are now routinely named as defendants in medical malpractice actions under a variety of theories of liability.

In addition to duty, in order to recover in a medical malpractice action, the patient must also establish that: (1) there was a breach of the duty owed the patient; (2) the health care provider's breach caused harm to the patient; and (3) that the patient sustained a compensable injury.

Medical negligence litigation is discussed more fully in Chapter 6 of this Almanac.

Liability for Employees and Attending Physicians

Whether the hospital is liable for medical negligence depends on the hospital's relationship with the health care provider who rendered the treatment.

The Doctrine of Respondeat Superior

Hospitals have historically enjoyed limited liability under malpractice law insofar as they were not liable for the acts of the physicians who used their facilities to treat patients. However, under the doctrine of "respondeat superior," hospitals have been deemed vicariously liable for the negligence of their own employees.

Employees

For a hospital to be vicariously liable for an employee, the employee must have been acting within the scope of his or her employment. The hospital would not generally be liable for intentional acts of an employee, unless the particular act was foreseeable.

Under the doctrine of *respondeat superior*, hospitals have been deemed vicariously liable for the negligence of their residents, interns and nurses. Further, in *Bing v. Thunig*, 2 N.Y.2d 656, 163 N.Y.S.2d 3, 143 N.E.2d 3 (1957), the New York Court of Appeals rejected a hospital exception to the *respondeat superior* doctrine, and found that physician *employees* are servants for this purpose as well.

Nevertheless, although many jurisdictions, such as New York, have rejected this exception to the *respondeat superior* doctrine, some courts are still reluctant to hold a hospital vicariously liable for the actions of staff physicians. Thus, the reader is advised to check the law of his or her own jurisdiction to determine hospital liability for its staff physicians.

Attending Physicians

Historically, hospitals have enjoyed limited liability and exposure in connection with the medical negligence of attending physicians who use their facilities to treat their private patients. This was based on the nature of the relationship between the hospital and the physician, and the view that the hospital was merely a "hotel" which provided facilities for the patients of the physicians to whom it grants privileges to practice.

A hospital will generally assert that the *respondeat superior* doctrine does not apply to an attending physician because he or she is an independent contractor and not an employee. Nevertheless, as discussed below, a hospital may still be found liable for its own independent negligence in selecting and granting privileges to an incompetent physician.

Corporate Negligence Doctrine

The corporate negligence doctrine has developed in response to the limited liability enjoyed by a hospital concerning the negligent care rendered by an attending physician who uses hospital facilities. The corporate negligence doctrine seeks to hold hospitals, as corporations, liable for their own independent negligence based on the breach of a duty owed "directly" to the patient.

Under the corporate negligence doctrine, a hospital is obligated to use reasonable care in granting privileges to an attending physician. Thus, if a hospital failed to properly investigate the credentials of an attending physician before granting them privileges, or if a hospital knew or should have known that the physician was incompetent based on its information, the hospital may be liable for negligently granting privileges.

For example, if the hospital did not use reasonable care in its review of the physician's credentials as an obstetrician, it may be subject to liability if the physician did not, in fact, have the proper credentials to practice this particular specialty and, in doing so, injured a patient.

Similarly, the hospital's medical staff has an assumed duty to supervise its staff physicians. Thus, if a staff physician acted negligently, and the medical staff failed to take any action against the physician, the hospital may be independently liable for negligent supervision and retention of the incompetent staff physician.

Other Bases for Independent Hospital Liability

A hospital may also be independently liable if its own employees fail to follow a private attending physician's orders. For example, hospital employees, such as nurses, are not permitted to supersede the course of treatment established by the private attending physician However, hospital liability may also arise if the private attending physician's course of treatment is clearly contraindicated, and hospital employees do not make a reasonable inquiry of the physician as to his treatment plan.

The hospital also has a duty of care owed directly to its patients that is independent of any duty owed the patient by the attending physician. For example, hospital employees are obligated to observe and record the condition of its patients so that the attending physician may render the appropriate treatment.

Other independent duties which Courts have determined give rise to hospital liability include the duty to protect the patient from harm; the duty to adequately perform clinical tests; the duty to keep accurate medical records; and the duty to properly admit and discharge a patient.

Joint and Several Liability

The defendant hospital may attempt to shift blame to a co-defendant, such as a private attending physician, to escape liability. However, the doctrine of joint and several liability may be imposed when multiple parties are responsible for the plaintiff's injury.

Case law has held that when two defendants are both negligent, but only one of them could have caused the plaintiff's injury, the court will hold both of them liable if it cannot determine which of the defendants caused the damage.

In such a case, it is the defendants who must come forward with evidence to absolve themselves. This shifts the burden of proof to the defendants. Otherwise, the plaintiff would never be able to prove who actually caused the injury.

Some states have enacted comparative negligence statutes that limit the recovery among multiple defendants to the amount of their proportional responsibility for the injury.

A table of state statutes governing joint and several liability in medical malpractice cases is set forth in Appendix 6.

Governmental Immunity

Historically, hospitals that were owned and operated by federal and state governments were immune from civil liability under the sovereignty doctrine that evolved from the English common law. The sovereignty doctrine provides that federal and state governments are supreme and, thus, government agents and employees are immune from lawsuits.

Nevertheless, the immunities previously enjoyed by the federal government and many state governments have for the most part been limited or abolished by statute and case law. For example, the Federal Tort Claims Act (FTCA) allows the federal government to be sued for the negligence of its employee acting within the scope of his or her employment. However, the federal government would not be liable for the negligence of independent contractors. It is incumbent upon the plaintiff to prove the employment status of the wrongdoer.

Nevertheless, the immunity doctrine still applies to intentional torts. For example, a claim of "battery" based on lack of consent for a particular medical procedure is an intentional act and would not be permitted under the FTCA. Lawsuits under the FTCA must be brought in the federal district court that maintains exclusive jurisdiction over such actions.

Similarly, many states have enacted legislation to allow injured individuals to obtain compensation. Nevertheless, some form of the immunity doctrine may still prevail in a minority of states.

For example, some states have placed monetary limits on the damages recoverable in a medical negligence case. Thus, the reader is advised to check the law of his or her own jurisdiction to determine whether a governmental immunity exists, and the extent of the immunity.

A table of state statutes governing limits on damage awards in medical malpractice cases is set forth in Appendix 7.

CHAPTER 4:
UNDERSTANDING THE HOSPITAL
RECORD

THE PATIENT'S RIGHT TO ACCESS MEDICAL RECORDS

The patient has an absolute right to obtain a copy of his or her medical record. There are a number of circumstances under which an individual might need those records. In preparing a medical negligence case against a hospital, physician, or other health care provider, one must first obtain all relevant medical records for review.

For example, if the patient believes their treatment by a certain medical provider was below acceptable standards, and they suffered injuries as a result, they may retain a medical expert to review the records to determine whether their care and treatment deviated from acceptable standards of medical practice.

In addition, an individual may want to obtain their records to get a second opinion before undergoing medical treatment. One may also need access to your medical records in connection with disability proceedings, insurance applications, and when changing medical providers.

ACCESSING MEDICAL RECORDS

In order to obtain a copy of a patient's medical record, an authorization for the release of the records must be signed by the patient or, in the case of a minor, by his or her parent or legal guardian. The release is then sent to the medical records department of the hospital or other health care provider. The authorization must contain the information required under the Health Insurance Portability and Accountability Act (HIPAA), as discussed more fully in Chapter 7, "The HIPAA Privacy Rule," of this Almanac.

The hospital or health care provider is entitled to charge a reasonable fee for copying and mailing the records. Some hospitals hire outside companies to undertake the task of copying the records and billing the patient. Generally, the patient receives copies of the medical records once the costs are submitted.

Many jurisdictions place a statutory cap on the amount a health care provider may charge for copying the records. For example, in New York, the Public Health Law limits the fee to 75 cents per page. The reader is advised to check the law of his or her jurisdiction concerning the applicable fee.

ELEMENTS OF THE HOSPITAL RECORD

In General

A patient's hospital record generally includes all records related to the individual's care and treatment while a patient in the hospital. A patient's medical records come in a number of different formats, most typically as paper documents and x-rays. However, other formats, such as nuclear medicine test results, magnetic resonance imaging (MRI) scans, digital mammography studies, or a doctor's dictation also exist and would be considered part of the patient's medical records. In addition, certain electronic records may be included as a patient's hospital record.

Certain medical records are generally not considered part of a patient's medical record, including but not limited to mental illness treatment records, alcohol and drug dependence treatment records, developmental disability treatment records, and certain HIV test results. A complete hospital record generally includes the materials set forth below.

Certification

Upon request, an authorized employee of the hospital's Medical Records Department will provide a signed document certifying that the copy of the hospital record has been compared with the original and is a true and complete copy. The certification may be used in support of having the medical record introduced as evidence in court.

Physician Attestation Statement

The physician attestation statement—also known as the identification sheet—is usually the first page of the hospital record. This document generally contains admission and discharge information, and is signed by a physician.

The admission information usually consists of the patient's background and insurance information, and the admitting diagnosis. Upon discharge, this document also sets forth the final diagnosis, any complications and secondary diagnoses, and any procedures performed, including surgical procedures.

Admission Record

The admission record contains information about the patient's medical history and the findings of his or her physical examination upon admission, including the results of laboratory and other testing, such as x-rays and MRIs. This document also contains the history of the patient's present illness or injury, and the course of treatment to be followed.

Consent Forms

The hospital record includes any consent forms signed by the patient, including consent to treatment, surgery and anesthesia, and other procedures. The forms are generally filled out upon admission and at other times during the patient's hospitalization when a particular procedure may be required.

Progress Notes

The progress notes include the attending physician's chronological record of developments that occur during a patient's hospitalization. These notations are generally made during routine hospital rounds and upon any significant change in the patient's condition or treatment.

Nursing Notes and Flow Charts

Depending on the hospital, a nurse's progress notes may be contained within the physician's progress notes, or may be contained in a separate section known as a flow chart.

Nurse's notes generally include information and observations about the patient gathered during each shift, including the patient's physical, mental and emotional state; medications administered; vital signs such as blood pressure and pulse; food intake; personal hygiene and bathroom habits; any signification changes in the patient's condition; and discharge instructions and notes.

Doctor's Orders

The Doctor's Orders section of the hospital records contains the physician's instructions to the nursing staff concerning the patient's treatment and care, including medications and dosages; dietary requirements; and laboratory tests, etc.

Laboratory Reports

The laboratory reports may include blood and urine analyses; x-ray reports; MRI reports; electrocardiographs and the results of other diagnostic studies.

Requests for Consultation

The consultation request reports generally involve a request from the attending physician to another consulting physician for an opinion or some other assistance relating to the patient's treatment. The consulting physician will either enter his or her own report or add a notation to the attending physician's progress notes.

Discharge Summary

The discharge summary is the attending physician's overview of the patient's hospitalization and includes a restatement of the admitting history and physical examination, the patient's hospital course, diagnoses, results of diagnostic studies, treatment given, and disposition. The summary is generally dictated and transcribed on the day of discharge.

CORRECTING THE MEDICAL RECORD

If there are errors in one's medical records, a letter may be sent to the health care provider explaining the problem, and requesting that a correction be made to the records. The patient should also request that the letter be included in the patient's medical record.

Errors in medical transcription may occur. However, intentional falsification or destruction of a patient's medical records is illegal. If a patient suspects their medical records have been altered, destroyed, or the records are being withheld even after a signed release has been provided, the patient is advised to contact an attorney to discuss how to proceed.

EVALUATING MEDICAL RECORDS IN ANTICIPATION OF LITIGATION

A careful evaluation of all medical records, including the hospital record, is essential if a medical negligence action is going to be initiated. A necessary element in all medical negligence cases is a deviation from the standard of care, and the medical record is a primary source of such evidence.

A medical record may be very difficult to decipher for a layperson with no medical background. The handwriting is often illegible, and many notations are abbreviated. In addition, much of the medical terminology used in medical records is derived from Latin. Therefore, a working knowledge of medical terminology is helpful when reviewing medical records.

A table of commonly used medical terminology is set forth in Appendix 8.

CHAPTER 5:
ADVANCE HEALTH CARE DIRECTIVES

IN GENERAL

Every person has the right and responsibility to fully participate in all decisions related to their health care, including the right to refuse treatment. If there comes a point, however, that you are no longer able to make those important decisions—e.g., due to mental or physical incapacity—it is important to make sure that those decisions are made for you by those who you trust will act in your best interests, and according to your wishes.

This chapter discusses a patient's right to participate in their own health care decisions, and to execute advance health care directives in case he or she is unable, due to illness or incapacity, to make those decisions.

THE PATIENT'S RIGHT TO PARTICIPATE IN HEALTH CARE DECISIONS

If a patient is able to express his or her own decisions, the patient has the right to accept or refuse any medical treatment. However, the patient must be competent enough to understand the medical problem and the risks and benefits of the available treatment options.

Competency is a legal status imposed by the court. For example, minors are deemed legally incompetent to make decisions concerning their right to forego medical treatment.

The Patient's Right to Refuse Medical Treatment

An individual has a constitutional right to request the withdrawal or withholding of medical treatment, including the cessation of food and water, even if doing so will result in the person's death. Honoring a person's right to refuse medical treatment or other life sustaining intervention, especially at the end of life, is the most widely practiced and widely accepted "right to die" policy in our society.

Most states acknowledge that a competent adult has the legal right to refuse medical care. On the other hand, many states also set forth certain policy concerns—such as preservation of life and suicide prevention—to limit this right. The courts have looked to the circumstances concerning the patient when denial of the patient's rights is put in issue.

Generally, if the patient is capable of recovery, the state's interest in preserving life has more merit than when the patient is on his or her deathbed with no possibility of recovery. Further, the courts have distinguished between the act of suicide and the patient's right to die a natural death without being placed on life support.

States have also expressed concern over the impact refusal of medical treatment will have on innocent third parties—in particular, minor children. For example, certain religious groups hold that medical treatment—e.g., blood transfusions—violates their religious beliefs.

In these cases, the courts have generally held that a competent adult, without dependent children, may refuse treatment. However, if the refusal to have a critical blood transfusion will cause a single mother to die and leave her children orphaned, the court will likely order the parent to undergo the treatment.

The court will also usually order a pregnant woman to undergo treatment that is necessary to protect the unborn child.

Thus, where there is an overriding state concern, such as the protection of third parties, the adult may be compelled to accept the treatment.

A health care provider—e.g., on moral grounds—may not be able to accept the patient's wishes to forego necessary treatment. In that case, the health care provider should assist the patient in locating a health care provider who is able to care for the patient according to his or her wishes.

Some health care providers have raised concerns that withholding treatment is tantamount to abandonment. However, the courts have generally held that where treatment would be futile, terminating or withholding treatment is not abandonment. A commonly used guideline for deciding whether or not to withhold or withdraw medical treatments is called a "benefits and burdens assessment." A benefit refers to the successful outcome of a medical procedure or treatment.

The American Medical Association (AMA) Statement on Withholding or Withdrawing of Life-Prolonging Medical Treatment is set forth in Appendix 9 of this Almanac.

The Patient's Right to Refuse Life-Sustaining Treatment

A life-sustaining treatment has been defined to include any medical treatment, procedure, or intervention that, in the judgment of the attending physician, when applied to the patient, would serve only to prolong the dying process where the patient has a terminal illness or injury, or would serve only to maintain the patient in a condition of permanent unconsciousness.

Patients have the right to stop not only commonly recognized life-sustaining measures, such as assisted ventilation and cardiopulmonary resuscitation (CPR), but to also discontinue any other medical treatments that may prolong life, such as kidney dialysis, surgical procedures, blood transfusions, heart medication, antibiotics, etc., regardless of whether the refusal may result in death.

Nevertheless, life-sustaining treatment does not include symptomatic treatment, including the administration of medication or the performance of any medical treatment where, in the opinion of the attending physician, the medication or treatment is necessary to provide comfort or to alleviate pain, even if the pain medication has the effect of hastening their death. A patient's right to pain management is discussed below.

The Patient's Right to Refuse Nutrition and Hydration

Artificially provided nutrition and hydration refers to a medical treatment consisting of the administration of food and water through a tube or intravenous line, where the recipient is not required to chew or swallow voluntarily. Artificially provided nutrition and hydration does not include assisted feeding, such as spoon or bottle-feeding.

Do Not Resuscitate Order

A Do-Not-Resuscitate Order (DNR) is a physician's written order instructing health care providers not to attempt cardiopulmonary resuscitation (CPR) in the event the patient suffers cardiac or respiratory arrest. A person with a valid DNR order will not be given CPR under these circumstances. Although the DNR order is written at the request of a person or his or her family, it generally must be signed by a physician to be valid. A non-hospital DNR order is written for individuals who are at home and do not want to receive CPR.

A sample Do Not Resuscitate Order is set forth in Appendix 10 of this Almanac.

The Patient's Right to Pain Management

People who experience pain have the right to receive treatment to alleviate their pain even if the pain medication has the effect of hastening their death. Proper treatment of pain depends on the type, location and duration of the pain. Efforts to reduce or eliminate the pain may include evaluation and treatment by surgeons or other doctors who specialize in treating the part of the body that is believed to be the source of the pain.

In general, there are three classifications of pain:

1. Acute Pain—Acute pain is usually severe and lasts for short periods of time. It can come from an accident, the onset of illness or disease, or as a result of surgery. Usually, the pain indicates that the body's tissue has been injured. Acute pain usually disappears as healing occurs.

2. Chronic Pain—Chronic pain stays for a long period of time. Chronic pain often accompanies certain diseases and conditions such as arthritis, migraine headaches, cancer, or sensitivity from an old injury or surgery.

3. Intractable Pain—Intractable pain occurs because the cause of the pain cannot be removed or otherwise treated. Intractable pain remains even after reasonable efforts have been made to reduce or eliminate it.

People experiencing pain are entitled to participate fully in the decisions affecting their care, and give truly informed consent to the treatment plan their doctor recommends. Regardless of the recommended treatment, the health care provider is required to advise the patient of the risks and benefits of all available treatments, and the goals of treatment.

People in pain have the right to receive treatment for their pain. Pain treatment may involve the use of drug and non-drug therapies, often in combination. In addition, patients have the right to choose alternative treatments to manage their pain, including physical therapy, acupuncture, biofeedback/relaxation techniques, massage, chiropractic care, psychotherapy to help manage depression that may accompany chronic or intractable pain, hypnosis, and behavior modification.

After evaluating the patient's condition, the health care provider may prescribe stronger medication, such as anti-depressants, nerve block injections, or opiates. Opiates, also known as narcotics, include morphine, codeine, and percodan. If the doctor will not prescribe opiates, the patient has the right to be referred to a doctor who will prescribe this pain medication.

Treatment of Minors

Because minors are deemed legally incompetent to make decisions concerning their right to forego medical treatment, the minor's parents make the decisions on the minor's behalf. However, when a minor is in critical need of treatment but the parent—e.g., due to religious beliefs—will not consent, court orders are routinely granted to the health care provider to administer the treatment. In some cases, a guardian is appointed by the court to protect the child.

A health care provider who is faced with a life-threatening situation must render the necessary treatment to the minor despite the parent's wishes, and instruct the parents to obtain a court order immediately if they want to prevent such treatment.

In situations where the minor is in such a physical state that any attempt to sustain life would be futile and cruel, the courts have held that the parents and health care provider can mutually decide to withhold treatment without seeking a court order. Nevertheless, this law generally does not permit the withholding of food and water as a means to hasten death in the case of a minor.

Release From Liability

Most hospitals will require a patient, or his or her representative, to sign a document that releases the attending physician, the hospital and its employees from liability if treatment is withheld or withdrawn. The document generally states the circumstances of the patient's condition, e.g., brain death, etc., giving rise to the request to terminate treatment.

The release of liability document also references the patient's advance directives—e.g., the patient's living will and durable power of attorney for health care—as proof of the patient's desire to forego life sustaining procedures and his or her appointment of an agent to make this decision if he or she is unable to do so.

In a subsequent medical malpractice action, a defendant may set forth a defense alleging that the patient assumed the risk of non-treatment by virtue of the release of liability.

Nevertheless, a release from liability would not limit a health care provider's liability for negligence. If the release contained such a provision, it would likely be unenforceable on public policy grounds.

A sample release from liability for discontinuing life sustaining treatment is set forth in Appendix 11 of this Almanac.

ADVANCE DIRECTIVES

An advance health care directive ("advance directive") is a general term that refers to one's oral and written instructions about their future medical care, in the event that they become unconscious or too sick to express their intentions. Executing an advance directive gives an individual the opportunity to make his or her own end-of-life health care decisions long after he or she has lost the capacity to do so.

The opportunity to execute advance directives responds to the individual's wishes to have some control over his or her destiny. Advance directives respond to the individual's concern that medical technology will prolong their life long after any reasonable possibility of recovery has disappeared. Many people prefer to "die with dignity" rather than remain comatose in a hospital bed attached to life support equipment for an indefinite duration. Further, the emotional toll that such a scenario causes the patient's family is another important factor to be considered.

An advance directive authorizes the medical care provider to cease some or all of these life support measures. On the other hand, an advance directive may also be used to instruct the medical care provider to undertake certain life-sustaining treatments in certain defined circumstances. In short, it is about giving the patient the choice and the right to make these decisions.

As set forth below, a living will and a durable power of attorney for health care are the two primary types of advance directives in use today. A comprehensive Health Care Advance Directive combines both the living will and the durable power of attorney for health care into one document, along with any other instructions you want followed, such as your desire to make an anatomical gift.

Advance Directives Legislation

All 50 states and the District of Columbia have laws recognizing the patient's right to control his or her medical treatment, and the use of some type of advance directive. The availability and scope of the particular advance directive varies from state to state, therefore, the reader is advised to check the law of his or her jurisdiction for specific provisions. Thus far, no state has challenged an individual's advance health care directives, and many states have enacted statutes that explicitly allow advance directives.

In addition, case law has supported an individual's express wishes concerning end-of-life health care decisions. The problem arises when an individual has not expressed those wishes, in writing, leaving it to the court to decide, based on evidence, whether a patient would have wanted certain actions to be taken, such as removal of life support. The only health care directives that have thus far been outlawed in all states, except Oregon, concern assisted suicide and euthanasia.

All states have some requirements for the execution of advance directives. For example, most states require witnesses to the signing and/or notarization. If there are any such formalities, you must make sure you follow them so that your advance directives will be followed. When choosing witnesses, you should not use people who are related to you; potential claimants to your estate, including heirs and persons named in your will; or your health care providers.

As set forth above, the law regarding advance directives varies from state to state. Therefore, if you spend a lot of time in another state, e.g., you own a second home out-of-state—you may consider executing an advance directive according to the laws of the second state. It is also advisable to name a different health care agent who is readily available in the second state, if the need arises, as your chosen health care agent should reside close to the location where you are being treated.

The Living Will

A living will is a written declaration, directed to your physician, stating that you wish to forgo extraordinary treatment of a terminal illness, in order to die a natural death. A living will differs from an ordinary will in that a living will only specifies health care wishes whereas an ordinary will deals with the disposition of property upon your death.

Although living wills may not be statutorily recognized in all states, all 50 states and the District of Columbia have enacted laws providing for some type of living will, medical proxy, or health care durable power of attorney that governs the right of the patient, or the patient's designated representative, to make decisions about the patient's health care. Further, an individual has a constitutional right to execute a living will.

A sample Living Will is set forth in Appendix 12 of this Almanac.

Purpose

The purpose of a living will is to give a person the right to decide the manner in which they will be treated should they develop an incurable illness or enter a persistent vegetative state, and become unable to communicate their wishes at that time. Generally, a living will provides that no heroic measures should be taken to prolong the individual's life where there is no reasonable expectation of recovery. However, pain medication is still usually administered.

A living will also provides family and loved ones some guidance in making a very painful decision. Further, a living will allows a health care provider to withdraw or withhold life-support treatment without risking a medical malpractice lawsuit.

Requirements

There are certain requirements that must be met to ensure recognition of a living will.

Competency

Any adult over the age of 18 may execute a living will provided he or she is deemed to be competent, and acting of his or her own free will. If the individual is incapacitated at the time of the decision to provide, withhold, or withdraw life-sustaining treatment or artificially provided nutrition and hydration, a living will is generally presumed to be valid.

In the case of a minor, the minor's parents, or guardians appointed by the court, are generally relied upon by health-care providers as substitutes for the minor.

Diagnosis

In general, most states require that two physicians must diagnose the patient as terminally ill. Many states also provide that a living will is valid only if signed after the physician has informed the patient that he or she has an incurable illness. Before executing a living will, it is prudent to determine exactly what requirements are imposed in your state.

Form

A living will must be made in writing. There are many different living will forms available. There are official forms set forth in the state's living will statute, and unofficial forms created by state medical and bar associations, senior citizens' groups, and national right to die organizations, etc. Some states require the use of a statutory form for a living will to be valid.

Witnesses

A living will must be signed by the person executing the document—the "maker." Although state laws vary, living will statutes generally require that there be two witnesses to the maker's signature, neither of whom can be related to the maker or beneficiaries of his or her estate.

Medical Condition

A living will sets forth the medical condition under which the will would need to be consulted. A typical clause reads as follows:

1. If at any time I should have a terminal or incurable condition caused by injury, disease, or illness, certified to be terminal or incurable by at least two physicians, which within reasonable medical judgment would cause my death, and where the application of life-sustaining procedures would serve only to artificially prolong the moment of my death, I direct that such procedures be withheld or withdrawn, and that I be permitted to die with dignity.

2. If at any time I experience irreversible brain injury, or a disease, illness, or condition that results in my being in a permanent, irreversible vegetative or comatose state, and such injury, disease, illness, or condition would preclude any cognitive, meaningful, or functional future existence, I direct my physicians and any other attending nursing or health care personnel to allow me to die with dignity, even if that requires the withdrawal or withholding of nutrition or hydration and my death will follow such withdrawal or withholding.

Life-Sustaining Treatment

A typical living will sets forth the type of life-sustaining treatment that may be provided, withheld or withdrawn. Basically, there are three general choices you can make regarding life-sustaining measures. You can request that:

1. Your health care providers do everything within their power to keep you alive;

2. The only life-sustaining measures you desire are nutrition (food) and hydration (water);

3. All artificial life-sustaining treatment is withheld, including nutrition and hydration.

Although it is not necessary to include every possible procedure to be provided, most living wills contain a clause setting forth the individual's intentions as to whether or not a certain "life-sustaining procedure" should be provided, withheld, or withdrawn if the individual's medical condition deteriorates. A typical clause reads as follows:

It is my expressed intent that the term "life-sustaining procedures" shall include not only medical or surgical procedures or interventions that utilize mechanical or other artificial means to sustain, restore, or supplant a vital function, but also shall include the placement, withdrawal, withholding, or maintenance of nasogastric tubes, gastrostomy, intravenous lines, heart-lung resuscitation, antibiotics, kidney dialysis, chemotherapy, or any other artificial, surgical, or invasive means for nutritional support and/or hydration.

Pain medication, nutrition and hydration are still usually given unless the living will specifically states that such treatment should be withheld.

Pregnancy Exclusions

Many living will statutes contain a pregnancy exclusion that provides that life-sustaining measures will continue regardless of any directive to the contrary until the pregnancy is complete, and that the pregnancy automatically invalidates the advance directive. For example, Missouri's law states:

"[T]he declaration to withdraw or withhold treatment by a patient diagnosed as pregnant by the attending physician shall have no effect during the course of the declarant's pregnancy." [Missouri Revised Statutes §49.025]

Other states use a viability standard to determine the enforceability of the advance directive. For example, Colorado's law states:

"In the case of a declaration of a qualified patient known to the attending physician to be pregnant, a medical evaluation shall be made as to whether the fetus is viable and could with a reasonable degree of medical certainty develop to live birth with continued application of life-sustaining procedures. If such is the case, the declaration shall be given no force or effect." [Colorado Medical Treatment Decision Act §15-18-104(2)].

A number of states are silent on the issue of pregnancy as it relates to a declaration contained in a living will. When a statute is silent, a court may be asked to decide whether the terms of the patient's living will would override the pregnancy. The court may hear testimony on this issue consisting of a patient's prior statements and conversations, to make its determination.

Amending or Revoking Your Living Will

As with any advance health care directive, you can amend your living will at any time, provided you are of sound mind and acting of your own free will. You may also revoke or terminate an existing living will without creating a new one.

If you choose to amend your living will, and the changes you wish to make are minor, you should put the changes in writing, sign and date the amendment, and have it witnessed. Attach the amendment to your original living will and make sure all persons who received a copy also receive the amendment.

If the changes you want to make are significant, it is advisable to start from the beginning and re-write your living will. Sign and date the new living will, have it witnessed, and provide a copy to everyone who was given copies of your prior living will.

Durable Power of Attorney for Health Care

In order to have your wishes concerning medical treatment known and honored should you become incapacitated, you can designate a health care agent by executing what is generally known as a durable power of attorney for health care, also known as a "health care proxy" in some jurisdictions. In effect, the person you appoint "stands in your shoes" for the purposes of making your health care decisions.

Purpose

Both the living will and the durable power of attorney are types of advance directives, however, they serve two different purposes. The living will, which was developed before the durable power of attorney for health care, sets forth the patient's intentions in case of terminal illness or persistent unconsciousness. A durable power of attorney authorizes a health care agent to make health care decisions for the patient when he or she is no longer capable of making them.

A sample Durable Power of Attorney for Health Care is set forth in Appendix 13 of this Almanac.

Persons Authorized to Make Health Care Decisions

The individual is always the dominant source for health care decision-making. Even if another person assumes the decision-making role as agent, guardian, or surrogate, the decision-maker must always follow the individual's instructions.

Health Care Agent

As set forth above, an adult or emancipated minor may execute a durable power of attorney for health care and authorize a health care agent to make any health care decisions that he or she could have made while having capacity. Therefore, the appointment of a health care agent must be made very carefully.

In general, a designation of health care agent must be accepted in writing by the person designated to serve in that capacity. Therefore, it is important that you discuss your wishes thoroughly with the person you intend to appoint. You must make sure the person you appoint is comfortable with the directives contained in your living will, and is willing and able to carry out your wishes. The individual must be made aware that they could be called upon to discontinue life-sustaining procedures, and must be willing to take on this responsibility.

Alternate Health Care Agent

It is generally undesirable to appoint a "co-health care agent" as this can lead to disagreements and delays. However, you should designate one or two alternate health care agents. If your first choice for health care agent is not available, or unable to act when health care decisions must be made, the alternate health care agent is called upon to make your health care decisions. Otherwise, health care providers will make treatment decisions for you that follow instructions you gave while you were still able to do so. Any instructions that you write in your living will or durable power of attorney will guide health care providers under these circumstances.

Court-Appointed Guardian

If a guardian has been appointed by the court for the patient, the guardian may not revoke the health care agent's authority unless the court specifically authorizes a revocation. The health care agent's decision under an unrevoked power of attorney takes precedence over the guardian's decision. However, if there is no health care agent appointed, a guardian may make health-care decisions on behalf of the patient.

Surrogate

If the patient has not appointed a health care agent, and there is no court-appointed guardian, a surrogate may assume the authority to make health care decisions for the patient in the same manner as a health care agent under a durable power of attorney. A patient selects a surrogate by advising his or her health care provider of their choice for surrogate.

Relative

If a patient does not select a surrogate to make his or her health care decisions, then an individual related to the patient can step forward and assume the authority. Following is a list of family members, in priority order, who are generally authorized to make health care decisions of a patient if the patient did not select a health care agent or surrogate:

1. Spouse

2. Adult child

3. Parent

4. Adult brother or sister

If there is no available relative, the authority to make health care decisions for the patient may be assumed by an adult who has exhibited special care and concern for the patient, who is familiar with the patient's personal values, and who is willing and able to make a health care decision for the patient.

If the health care provider is unable to find any person who can qualify as a surrogate, the health care provider may ask a court to appoint a surrogate to make health care decisions for the patient.

Exclusions

Most states exclude the following people from appointment as a patient's health care agent:

1. The patient's doctor or other treating health care provider;

2. A non-relative employee of the patient's hospital or health care provider;

3. An operator of the patient's nursing home or assisted living facility;

4. A non-relative employee of the patient's nursing home or assisted living facility.

In addition, in some states, the divorce, dissolution, or annulment of the patient's marriage revokes the designation of the patient's former spouse as health care agent. If, following divorce, dissolution or annulment of the patient's marriage, the patient still desires a former spouse to act as their health care agent, they must state their choice in their health care agent designation, or in their order of divorce, dissolution, or annulment of marriage.

Treatment Decisions

The health care agent must make decisions regarding the providing, withholding, or withdrawing of life-sustaining treatment or artificially provided nutrition and hydration according to the patient's specific instructions contained in the patient's living will, if one was executed, or other instructions.

If there are no specific directions concerning a certain course of treatment, the health care agent's decisions must conform as closely as possible to what the patient would have wanted under the circumstances. The health care agent must take into account the patient's personal beliefs, moral values, religious view, etc.

The health care agent exercises a lot of control over your health care and possible outcome if you become incapacitated. Thus, in writing your durable power of attorney, you must consider the scope of your health care agent's authority. You can limit your health care agent's authority, or you can give your health care agent very broad authority.

In general, you can give your health care agent the authority to:

1. Consent to, or refuse, medical treatment and procedures;

2. Employ or dismiss your health care providers;

3. Choose your health care facility;

4. Access your medical records;

5. Consent to pain and comfort medication;

6. Withhold hydration and nutrition; and

7. Take any other steps necessary to carry out your health care instructions.

However, unless your living will specifically provides that nutrition and hydration may be withdrawn or withheld, the health care agent is generally not permitted to make this decision

Making Sure Your Wishes Are Followed

Most hospitals will allow you to keep a copy of your advance directives on file with them. Therefore, it is important to check with your hospital to make sure your advance directive documents conform to their requirements. If a hospital has a policy against advance directives, it is required to advise you at the time you are admitted.

You should also discuss your advance directives with your physician, particularly since a physician does not have the same obligation to inform you as a hospital does, therefore, you should inquire about any such policy up front.

If your physician or your hospital appears to be unwilling to comply with your wishes—e.g., on religious grounds—you should consider finding alternative medical care as soon as possible. In most states, a health care provider who refuses to honor a patient's health care advance directive is required to make reasonable efforts to transfer the patient to another health care provider who will comply.

Also discuss this matter with your family, so that they will be prepared if called on to support your decision. You must make your wishes known ahead of time to ensure that they will be followed.

You should keep the original health care directive in a place where it will easily be found in case you are unable to communicate. Copies should be given to your health care agent, your physician, designated hospitals or health care facilities, your minister or other religious advisor, certain family members, and your attorney. You may also carry a card with you, similar to an organ donor card, which contains basic information about the existence of your health care directives and contact information.

Your health care directive should be reviewed periodically, e.g., every five to ten years, depending on your age. You should also consider amending the document after certain events, such as marriage, divorce, retirement, diagnosis of illness, etc.

Some state statutes have made it a crime to falsify or forge a patient's advance health care directive, or to willfully conceal or withhold personal knowledge of the revocation of an advance directive. And, it is a felony if done with the intent to cause the withholding or withdrawal of life-sustaining treatment, or to artificially provide nutrition and hydration, contrary to the individual's wishes, and those actions hasten the patient's death.

Medical Battery

A health care provider who imposes medical treatment contrary to the instructions left in an advance directive may be guilty of medical battery. Claims of battery against physicians for nonconsensual medical care have been recognized for some time even if the medical procedure is harmless, beneficial, or life-sustaining. The courts are becoming increasingly willing to find that battery has occurred in cases in which a health care provider refused to honor the directions left in an advance directive or given by an appointed agent.

Combining Your Living Will with a Health Care Proxy

Most states allow for a living will and a durable power of attorney to be combined into one document. However, if you execute both a living will and a durable power of attorney for health care, you must make sure that the terms of both documents are consistent to avoid confusion or invalidation. Discuss this matter with your physician and provide your physician with a copy of your documents.

THE PATIENT SELF-DETERMINATION ACT

In General

The Patient Self-Determination Act (PSDA) is a federal law that was passed by the U.S. Congress in 1990 and went into effect on December 1, 1991. The PSDA does not afford patients any new rights. It is the requirement that health care facilities advise patients of their already existing rights that makes this law so important.

Prior to enactment of the PSDA, many patients were unaware of their right to receive information that would help them make important decisions concerning their health care. Every individual has certain constitutionally protected rights regarding health care, such as the right to consent to, or refuse, treatment.

The intent of the PSDA is to make sure patients are able to protect these rights in case they become at some point unable to do so, thus allowing the individual to maintain control of his or her own health care choices to the greatest extent possible.

Covered Institutions

The PSDA governs virtually all health care facilities that receive Medicare or Medicaid funding, including hospitals, skilled nursing facilities, extended care facilities, hospice programs, health maintenance organizations, and home health care agencies. The only facilities that are exempt from the law are those institutions where the patients pay for their own health care services without any government assistance. This ensures that most individuals who receive health care will be covered by the law.

Requirements of the PSDA

There are three important provisions of the PSDA detailing the obligations of: (1) covered health care facilities; (2) the individual states; and (3) the Secretary of the Department of Health and Human Services, as set forth below.

Health Care Facilities

The PSDA is based on the concept of informed consent. Under the PSDA, covered health care facilities are required to give their patients information on applicable state laws regarding advance health care directives. An advance directive refers to a written instruction executed by an individual which relates to the provision of health care should that individual become incapacitated, such as a living will or durable power of attorney for health care.

To comply with the PSDA requirements, patients must be given written information, upon admission to the facility, explaining their right to execute advance directives concerning their end-of-life care, and their right to participate in the decisions affecting their health care, including the following:

    1. The patient's right to accept or refuse treatment;

2. The patient's rights under existing state laws, whether statutory or judge-made, regarding their right to formalize advance directives; and

3. Information concerning any written policies that the institution has concerning the implementation of the patient's rights.

The health care facility is also required to document each patient's medical record concerning the existence of any advance directives executed by the patient. Nevertheless, health care providers are expressly prohibited from conditioning the provision of care, or from otherwise discriminating against the patient, based on whether or not the individual has executed an advance directive.

In addition to the requirement to provide information to the patient, covered health care facilities must engage in ongoing educational activities for both their staff and the community on issues concerning advance directives, including the right to accept or refuse treatment and the opportunity for drafting or signing advance directives.

The PSDA also sets forth the time at which the patient is to receive the advance directives information, depending on the type of covered health care facility, as follows:

1. A hospital is required to provide the patient with this information at the time he or she is admitted as an inpatient.

2. A skilled nursing facility is required to provide the patient with this information at the time he or she is admitted as a resident.

3. Home health agencies are required to provide the patient with this information prior to the time the individual comes under the care of the agency.

4. Hospice programs are required to provide the patient with this information at the time hospice care is initiated.

5. Health maintenance organizations are required to provide the patient with this information at the time he or she enrolls in the plan.

In addition, the advance directives information must be provided to the patient each time he or she is admitted and/or comes under the care of a particular facility. For example, if an individual is first admitted to a hospital and then later transferred to a nursing home, both the hospital and the nursing home are required to independently provide the advance directives information to the individual upon admission.

Individual States

The PSDA requires each individual state to develop a written description of its law, whether statutory or judge-made, concerning the advanced directives that would be distributed by covered health care facilities.

Secretary of the Department of Health and Human Services

The PSDA requires the Secretary of the Department of Health and Human Services to:

1. Develop and implement a national campaign to inform the public of the option to execute advance directives, and of a patient's right to participate in, and control, his or her own health care decisions; and

2. Develop or approve nationwide information materials, to be distributed by health care providers, which would:

(a) inform the public and the medical and legal profession of the individual's right to make decisions concerning their medical care, including the right to accept or refuse treatment; and

(b) inform the public and the medical and legal profession of the existence of advance directives.

In addition, the Secretary is required to work with the individual states in preparing material concerning applicable state laws on the subject, to mail such information to all recipients of social security, and to include information concerning the PSDA in the Medicare handbook.

The Patient Self-Determination Act is set forth in Appendix 14 of this Almanac.

THE UNIFORM HEALTH CARE DECISIONS ACT

In 1982, the National Conference of Commissioners on Uniform State Laws (NCCUSL) promulgated the Model Health-Care Consent Act, which addressed the broad issues of consent to treatment, but the Act did not address end-of-life decisions for terminal patients. The NCCUSL subsequently drafted the Uniform Rights of the Terminally Ill Act in 1985, amended in 1989, to address the narrower issues of dying patients.

Since that time, every state has enacted the use of some sort of advance health care directive, and most states have statutorily authorized the living will and the durable power of attorney for health care. However, there still exists inconsistency among state laws, which leads to conflict when an advance directive executed in one state must be implemented in another state.

Recognizing this problem, and the need for uniformity among state laws, in 1993, the NCCUSL drafted the Health Care Decisions Act. The Act is comprehensive and is designed to replace existing legislation concerning advance directives—e.g., living will, power of attorney and family consent statutes, etc.—with one all-encompassing statute.

The Act is endorsed by the American Bar Association (ABA) and the American Association of Retired Persons (AARP), and has been adopted by Alabama, Alaska, Delaware, Hawaii, Maine, Mississippi, New Mexico, and Wyoming.

Patient's Rights

The Act acknowledges the right of a competent individual to decide all aspects of his or her own health care in all circumstances, including the right to refuse health care, or to withhold or withdraw treatment, even if it results in the patient's death. The Act also recognizes the individual's right to appoint a health care agent to carry out his or her wishes if the patient is incapacitated and unable to communicate his or her wishes.

Authorization of Health Care Decision Makers

The Act authorizes designated health care agents to make health care decisions for a patient who cannot or does not wish to make such decisions. The Act also authorizes a designated surrogate, family member, or close friend to make such decisions when a guardian or health care agent has not been appointed or is not available to serve in that capacity. If there is no person appointed or available to make health care decisions, the Act authorizes such decisions to be made by the appropriate court.

Form of Advance Directives

The Act simplifies and facilitates the drafting of advance health care directives. Under the Act, a health care instruction may be given orally or in writing. Further, a durable power of attorney for health care need not be witnessed or acknowledged, although the document must be in writing. The Act also sets forth a form of advance health care directive, the use of which is optional.

Patient's Instructions

The goal of the Act is to make sure that the patient's wishes concerning his or her health care are carried out. If the patient is incapacitated or otherwise unable to express those wishes, an authorized agent must make health care decisions in accordance with the patient's instructions to the extent known or, if unknown, in accordance with the best interests of the patient.

Compliance Requirements

The Act requires health care providers and institutions to comply with the patient's instructions, however, a health care provider or institution may decline to honor an instruction or decision for reasons of conscience or if the instruction or decision requires the provision of medically ineffective care or care contrary to applicable health-care standards. Nevertheless, the health care provider or institution must make a reasonable effort to transfer the patient to the care of a provider who will comply.

Under the Act, when a health care provider complies with the Act in good faith, the health care provider has immunity from prosecution and/or civil liability, even if the provider withdraws treatment that prolongs life.

Validity of Out-of-State Advance Health Care Directives

An important provision of the Act is that it ensures the validity of an advance health care directive regardless of when or where executed or communicated, thus an advance directive drafted in one state will be valid in any state that has adopted the Act.

Dispute Resolution

The Act sets forth a dispute resolution procedure and also authorizes a court to either enjoin or order a health care decision.

The Uniform Health Care Decisions Act is set forth in Appendix 15.

CHAPTER 6:
MEDICAL NEGLIGENCE LITIGATION

IN GENERAL

Historically, patients have relied on the advice of their medical providers with few, if any, questions asked. It was assumed that the doctor was the expert and knew what was best for the patient. Although the majority of health care providers are competent professionals with the utmost concern for the well-being of their patients, medical mistakes do occur.

Nevertheless, not every medical mistake qualifies as actionable medical malpractice. Medical malpractice involves the commission of a tort—a wrongful act—as do all personal injury actions. However, there are a number of differences unique to medical negligence litigation, and the standards of proof are much higher than in a simple negligence case.

In addition, largely due to the power and support behind the health care industry, lawyers for this powerful industry have been successful in passing legislation designed to reduce medical negligence litigation. Such legislation includes shortened statutes of limitations in medical negligence cases, limits on damage awards, and the placement of caps on legal fees in an effort to dissuade lawyers from taking on such cases. Some states require the lawyer to prove the merits of a case even before the action can be filed.

Unfortunately, such restrictive legislation does little to reduce medical negligence and promote patient safety. Thus, the primary incentive for improving the quality of health care is through successful medical malpractice litigation and large monetary awards. In the meantime, the public must be made aware of the ways they can try and protect themselves from medical negligence before it occurs.

THE MEDICAL NEGLIGENCE ATTORNEY

To find out whether there are grounds to bring a medical negligence action, an injured patient should meet with an attorney to discuss the facts and allegations concerning the client's claim. In considering whether to take the case, the attorney will generally request all of the plaintiff's medical records, including prescriptions and billing records. The attorney may also have the prospective client's medical records reviewed by a physician to determine whether the case has merit.

If the attorney agrees to take the case, the client will be required to sign a retainer agreement which sets forth the terms of compensation, costs and services to be provided. In states where legal fees are limited by statute, the legal fees set forth in the retainer agreement should reflect those limits.

A table of state statutes governing attorney fees in medical malpractice cases is set forth in Appendix 16.

Medical malpractice cases are generally taken on a contingency fee basis. This means that the attorney does not receive a legal fee unless there is a recovery. An attorney may also be retained on an hourly fee basis, however, on that basis, the client would be required to pay the attorney's fee whether or not there is a successful outcome.

The client is also generally responsible for the payment of disbursements— e.g., court filing fees, expert witness fees, etc.—despite the outcome of the case. However, most attorneys will advance those costs and seek reimbursement from the recovery, if any.

INVESTIGATING THE BACKGROUND OF THE DEFENDANT

As more fully discussed in Chapter 2, "Protecting Yourself from Medical Mistakes," an investigation into the background of the defendant health care provider—i.e., the hospital and/or medical personnel— should be undertaken in preparation for litigation.

Sources of information include state licensing agencies, medical boards, and medical and/or other professional schools the defendant may have attended. An investigation of court files to see whether the defendant has ever been sued before may provide important information.

DETERMINING THE STATUTE OF LIMITATIONS

The statute of limitations refers to any law that sets forth a time period within which a claimant must bring a lawsuit to avoid being barred from enforcing a right or claim. Filing an action beyond the statute of limitations is a common defense in all litigation.

Most jurisdictions have shortened the statute of limitations as it applies to medical malpractice claims. The case must be filed before the expiration date or risk dismissal. The statute generally begins to run from the date of injury, discovery of the injury, or the date that the injury should reasonably have been discovered.

Nevertheless, the statute of limitations may be tolled—that is, suspended—under certain circumstances, such as in situations where there has been intentional concealment or fraud on the part of the defendant, or where a foreign object is discovered in the patient's body. The statute may also be tolled when there exists a statutory disability to bringing the action, such as infancy.

A table of state statutes of limitations in medical malpractice cases is set forth in Appendix 17.

INITIATING THE LAWSUIT

The Summons and Complaint

The medical malpractice lawsuit is officially begun when service of a summons and complaint is made upon the defendant. The complaint details the plaintiff's malpractice claim against the defendant, and sets forth the legal theory under which the plaintiff seeks to prevail. The plaintiff may set forth more than one legal theory. For example, common medical malpractice allegations may include negligence, lack of informed consent, and breach of contract.

The plaintiff must be able to prove the essential elements of the theory set forth in the complaint in order to prevail. In addition, as set forth below, the lawsuit must be filed within the statutorily prescribed period of time for medical malpractice actions. This time period is referred to as the statute of limitations.

The Certificate of Merit

States that require a showing of merit in order to file the action generally require that a physician review the records and indicate to the attorney that there appears to be some departure from accepted medical practices.

Depending on the state, the attorney may be required to file a certificate of merit which states that the attorney has consulted with a physician and, based upon that consultation, the action has merit.

THE DEFENDANT'S RESPONSE

The Answer

Upon receipt of the summons and complaint, the defendant must respond to the complaint within a prescribed period of time or risk losing the dispute by default. The defendant may serve an answer to the complaint, or may choose to make a motion seeking to dismiss the complaint prior to serving his or her answer.

These preliminary motions are usually based on some technical point, such as improper service or lack of jurisdiction. If the motion is granted, the case is dismissed. However, if the motion is denied, the defendant must serve an answer within a statutorily defined time period following the decision on the motion.

The defendant's answer admits or denies the allegations set forth in the complaint. The defendant may also assert counterclaims in his or her answer that must in turn be "answered" by the plaintiff in a formal response within a prescribed period of time. The defendant's answer will also present any defenses to the allegations that the defendant may have, which commonly include defenses based on: (i) the statute of limitations; and (ii) contributory fault of the plaintiff.

Contributory Fault

The defendant may allege as a defense that the plaintiff's own actions contributed in some way to his or her injury. For example, if the patient failed to take the prescribed medication to treat his or her condition, depending on the jurisdiction, the plaintiff's contributory negligence may be a complete bar to recovery.

Most jurisdictions, however, have enacted comparative negligence statutes as an alternative to the harshness of the recovery rules of contributory negligence. Under comparative negligence, the plaintiff's recovery may be diminished, but only according to the plaintiff's degree of culpability.

DISCOVERY PROCEEDINGS

Medical malpractice litigation generally involves a lengthy discovery process. Typical discovery may include the exchange of detailed information, the examination of documents and other evidence, and an oral examination of the parties and prospective witnesses in a proceeding known as a deposition or examination before trial, depending on the jurisdiction.

During a deposition, the deponent is placed under oath, and must answer a series of questions put forth by the parties or their attorneys. The sworn testimony given at the deposition is recorded by a legal stenographer, who prepares a transcript of the testimony for use at trial. The deposition testimony pins down each deponent's version of the facts, and can be used to impeach a party or non-party witness.

MOTION PRACTICE

The litigation procedure, from initiation of the lawsuit to final disposition, is governed by the statutory law of the particular court in which the lawsuit is filed. During the pendency of the lawsuit, much of litigation is accomplished on paper. There are numerous motions that a party may file and ask the assigned judge to rule upon. A motion, which may be made orally or in writing, is an application to the court requesting an order or a ruling in favor of the applicant.

For example, a party may make a motion seeking some type of interim relief, such as the production of certain evidence. The notice of motion and any supporting papers are served upon the other party, who usually responds in opposition to the motion.

THE TRIAL

As the trial date approaches, the judge will usually set the matter down for a pretrial settlement conference, in an attempt to resolve the dispute without going to trial. Absent a successful settlement, the lawsuit eventually goes to trial, where the parties present their evidence. In order to recover at trial, the plaintiff must establish the following elements:

1. The existence of the health care provider's duty to the plaintiff—that is, the health care provider/patient relationship;

2. The applicable standard of care and the health care provider's violation of that standard;

3. A compensable injury; and

4. A causal connection between the health care provider's violation of the standard of care and the harm suffered.

At any time up to the announcement of the verdict, the parties may settle the action. In that case, the jury will be dismissed and the judge will generally enter the settlement on the record. The parties will execute a formal settlement agreement.

After the trial has concluded, assuming it has not been settled along the way, a decision is rendered by the factfinder—i.e., the judge or jury. The losing party may seek to appeal the unfavorable decision to a higher court. Once the appeals process has been exhausted, the decision is final and enforceable.

ESTABLISHING LIABILITY

Negligence is the predominant theory of medical malpractice litigation. In order to recover in a medical malpractice action, the plaintiff must establish the following elements:

1. Duty—The existence of the health care provider's duty to the plaintiff—i.e., the health care provider/patient relationship;

2. The Standard of Care—The applicable standard of care and the health care provider's deviation from that standard—i.e., the breach of duty;

3. A causal connection between the health care provider's violation of the standard of care and the harm suffered; and

4. A compensable injury—i.e., damages.

The Health Care Provider/Patient Relationship

Liability for medical malpractice cannot exist unless there is a health care provider/patient relationship that creates a duty on the part of the health care provider to render acceptable medical care to the patient. The health care provider/patient relationship is generally found to exist where the health care provider undertakes to treat the patient, thus creating a professional relationship.

The health care provider/patient relationship may also be based on a contract theory, in that the patient pays, or agrees to pay, the health care provider for his or her services.

Once the health care provider/patient relationship is deemed to have arisen, it cannot be unilaterally terminated by the health care provider without there being a mutual understanding by both health care provider and patient or the health care provider may be held liable for abandonment of the patient.

Termination of the relationship may result when:

1. The patient terminates the relationship; or

2. The treatment undertaken is completed and further treatment is no longer necessary; or

3. The health care provider notifies the patient that he or she can no longer render services to the patient and either (a) refers the patient

to another health care provider, or (b) extends a reasonable amount of time for the patient to find other suitable medical care.

The Standard of Care

In order to prevail in a lawsuit against a hospital, the plaintiff must show that the hospital did not comply with the applicable standard of care, and that the plaintiff's injuries were proximately caused by this deviation in the standard of care.

Case law has held that a hospital owes a duty to its patients to possess knowledge, and exercise that degree of care and skill, normally possessed by like institutions. However, the applicable standard of care for a hospital depends on whether the claims involve simple negligence or medical malpractice.

Simple Negligence

Simple negligence applies to non-medical, ministerial or administrative acts, and is judged by a "reasonable person" standard. Generally, the statute of limitations in a simple negligence case is longer than that based on medical malpractice.

Medical Malpractice

Unlike simple negligence, medical malpractice is judged by a comparative standard of conduct—i.e., the standard of care that is common to those who are recognized in the profession itself as qualified and competent to engage in it. Thus, as set forth in Section 299A of the Restatement of Torts, the standard of care for medical negligence is not that of the most highly skilled member of the profession, nor is it that of the average member of the profession. The medical negligence case is generally governed by a shortened statute of limitations.

Simple Negligence and Medical Malpractice Compared

Determining whether an action against a hospital is simple negligence or medical malpractice depends on the conduct giving rise to the claim. For example, if the lack of care is understandable by the finder of fact without the need for an expert witness—i.e., based upon common knowledge—the conduct would generally constitute simple negligence. If the conduct relates to the professional skill and judgment of a health care provider, it would sound in medical malpractice and would likely require expert testimony.

It is sometimes difficult, however, to distinguish between the two causes of action. A basic guideline to follow in determining the proper cause of action is to examine whether the act or omission complained of is connected with medical treatment. If so, it is more appropriately designated a medical malpractice claim.

The Locality Rule

In applying the comparative standard of medical negligence, a hospital historically was required to provide "that level of care and treatment commensurate with like institutions in the same *locality*." The reason for the locality rule was to make sure that a small rural hospital was not unfairly held up to the standard of a more technologically advanced urban facility.

This locality rule has been the subject of much criticism because it is very difficult for a plaintiff to obtain expert testimony from a physician who practices in the same locality where the malpractice occurred. In addition, critics maintain that medical negligence should not go unpunished simply because the treatment was consistent with medical care rendered in the locality.

In order to combat this reasoning, the plaintiff is advised to demonstrate that the existing standards in that locality are simply inappropriate and fall below any acceptable standard of care. In any event, because of the relative ease of modern-day travel, the differences between care rendered in rural versus urban hospitals has narrowed.

The National Standard

Many courts have rejected the locality rule in its entirety, opting to apply a national standard instead. The national standard requires the plaintiff to prove that the health care provider departed from the standards applicable to the average member of those in the profession who practice the same specialty.

It has been proposed that negligent acts by a hospital may also be judged by a national standard. However, some courts have rejected applying such general standards to a hospital, holding that the level of care is not comparable because hospitals differ in terms of resources, size of the facility, and type and availability of specialized equipment.

Nevertheless, proponents of the national standard still maintain that while the national standard may not be appropriate for negligent actions by a hospital which are non-medical in nature, the national standard should still apply to the acts of professional malpractice committed by the health care providers employed by the hospital.

Joint Commission Standards

The Joint Commission has promulgated comprehensive standards for hospitals that may serve as a measuring stick when trying to determine whether a hospital has deviated from an acceptable standard of care.

The Joint Commission's standards are set forth in its Comprehensive Accreditation Manual for Hospitals (CAMH), and set forth standards in the following areas:

1. Ethics, Rights and Responsibilities;

2. Provision of Care;

3. Medication Management;

4. Surveillance, Prevention and Control of Infection;

5. Leadership;

6. Management of Environment of Care;

7. Management of Human Resources;

8. Management of Information;

9. Medical Staff, including credentialing and appointment; and

10. Management of Care, Treatment and Services.

Expert Testimony

The burden of proving that medical care departed from acceptable standards rests with the plaintiff. Generally, such proof is necessarily demonstrated by the use of expert testimony. Expert testimony is introduced through the opinions of other health care providers qualified in the particular area of medicine, who review the case and state that the defendant rendered negligent care.

If the departure was so obvious that a layperson of common knowledge or experience could understand it, expert testimony may not be necessary. In addition, if the defendant has made statements of admission, such as that he or she made a mistake, these statements may be sufficient exceptions to the expert testimony requirement.

If the alleged deviation from the applicable standard of care requires expert testimony, according to Section 299A of the Restatement of Torts, the standard of care is not that of the most highly skilled member of the profession, nor is it that of the average member of the profession, but it is the standard of care that is common to those who are recognized in the profession itself as qualified and competent to engage in it.

For example, if the care rendered by the most highly skilled surgeon was used as the measuring stick for negligence, then the majority of surgeons would automatically be found liable. Further, a health care provider's skill may fall below the average member of the profession, yet the health care provider may still be deemed qualified and competent.

The plaintiff's medical expert is generally called upon to testify for several purposes in the medical malpractice action:

1. To establish the applicable standard of care and demonstrated how it was violated;

2. To establish a causal connection between the negligence and the injury; and

3. To establish the extent of the injury.

The expert witness must be found competent to render his or her opinion in the matter. Thus, the expert must demonstrate that he or she is familiar with the defendant health care provider's specialty area; the medical procedures involved; and the applicable standard of care.

That familiarity generally results from the expert's own professional experience in the field. Where the geographic locality of the standard of care is in issue, the expert must be familiar with that setting as well. Once it is found that the expert is competent to testify, the extent of his or her experience would go to the weight given the testimony.

Professional Standards

Another method of proving that a health care provider deviated from the applicable standard of care would be to examine hospital regulations, policies, bylaws, standards, health and hospital codes, state statutes and regulations, etc., to determine whether the health care provider complied with those standards of care.

Res Ipsa Loquitur

Some states permit the doctrine of *res ipsa loquitur* in medical malpractice actions as a means of shifting the burden of proof to the defendant. Under this doctrine, the plaintiff must submit evidence that the injury would not have occurred in the absence of negligence.

The elements of the doctrine of *res ipsa loquitur* are:

1. The injury does not normally occur in the absence of negligence;

2. The health care provider had exclusive control of the instrumentality or agency of the injury; and

3. The injuries were not caused by the plaintiff's own contributory fault.

Courts are generally reluctant to apply the *res ipsa loquitur* doctrine in a medical malpractice action unless the negligence is so obvious that it is unnecessary to require expert testimony regarding the standard of care and its breach by the defendant. The most common type of case where the doctrine has been applied is when a foreign object has been unintentionally left in a patient during surgery.

If the plaintiff was under the exclusive control and care of more than one health care provider, then all such persons would be named as defendants in the action as being jointly and severally liable. This puts pressure on each individual to place the blame where it is due to avoid his or her liability.

Proximate Cause

In addition to proving that there was a deviation in the standard of care, the plaintiff must also establish a *causal connection* between the health care provider's actions and the harm suffered. If the plaintiff cannot prove that the act of malpractice caused the injury, the defendant will prevail. Proximate causation must be rooted in fact—the cause-in-fact—and supported by a legal connection between the action and the injury.

If there was an independent, intervening cause that breaks the causal connection between the first health care provider's negligent act and the intervening act, then the first health care provider may be excused from liability. However, if the intervening act was foreseeable, it would not be sufficient to break the causal connection.

To determine causation, there are two common tests:

1. The "but for" test—If it can be proven that it was more probably true than not, that the patient's injury would not have occurred "but for" the defendant's actions, causation has been established under this test.

2. The "substantial factor" test—If it can be proven that the defendant's actions were a substantial factor in bringing about the injury, causation has been established under this test.

Damages

Once liability and causation has been established, the damages suffered by the injured person must be proven in order to recover. In medical negligence cases, as in all personal injury law, damages are usually measured in terms of monetary compensation. There are three categories of money damages recoverable in a personal injury case: (1) compensatory damages; (2) punitive damages; and (3) nominal damages.

Compensatory Damages

Compensatory damages represent an attempt to compensate the injured party for the actual harm he suffered, by awarding the amount of money necessary to restore the plaintiff to his pre-injury condition. Often, a complete restoration cannot be accomplished. Thus, damages would include the monetary value of the difference between the plaintiff's pre-injury and post-injury conditions.

It should be noted that, in medical negligence cases, the degree of the health care provider's negligence does not translate into the damage award. The damages are directly related to making the plaintiff "whole." The plaintiff is entitled to an award of damages that restores him or her to their pre-injury status, in terms of monetary compensation.

The general rule is "you take your patient as you find him or her." Thus, a health care provider who commits a minor negligent act may end up paying much more than one who commits a severely negligent act, depending on the patient's resulting status. Therefore, it is the harm suffered, and not the degree of negligence, which is taken into account in computing the damage award. Typical items included in compensatory damage awards include:

Medical Expenses

Medical expenses are the most concrete and objectively demonstrable items to identify. The expense must be reasonably related to the defendant's wrongful conduct.

Lost Earnings and Impairment of Earning Capacity

Lost earnings and impairment of earning capacity are the most justifiable element of a general compensatory damages award from a strictly economic point of view. Recovery is sought for:

1. The earnings actually lost up to the time of the trial or settlement; and

2. The diminution in the plaintiff's capacity to earn in the future.

Pain, Suffering, and Other Intangible Elements

Pain and suffering is the most difficult element of recovery to measure. This is a broad concept, which may include a number of more or less separate factors, the most common of which is the physical pain associated with the injury. Recovery for mental suffering associated with bodily disfigurement may also be included as an element of pain and suffering. Another element is the loss of enjoyment in relation to

The "Occurrence" Policy

An "occurrence" policy provides coverage for only those claims arising during the term of the policy regardless of when the claim is actually made. The latter is the preferred type of policy because some types of claims may not be made until many years after the policy has expired, such as in the case of a minor. In addition, an "occurrence" policy will cover claims made against individuals who are no longer employed by, or associated with, the hospital.

Conditions of Coverage

A liability insurance policy generally contains three conditions which must be met in order to be covered for a claim, including:

1. Timely notice of the occurrence giving rise to the claim;

2. Timely notice of the claim; and

3. The insured party's cooperation.

The purpose of the notice provisions is so that the insurance carrier can make an expeditious and thorough investigation of all of the facts and circumstances relating to the claim. The earlier the investigation begins, the fresher the recollection of key witnesses. A thorough investigation will also give the insurance carrier some idea of the potential exposure related to the claim.

Nevertheless, late notice does not automatically void coverage, particularly where the insured hospital has expended large sums of money in insurance premiums. If the insurance carrier is not seriously prejudiced by the late notice, its obligation to defend the hospital may, nevertheless, stand.

The Insurance Carrier's Duty to Defend

In addition to paying the losses related to a successfully litigated claim, up to the limit of the policy, the insurance carrier is also obligated to defend the hospital, including paying for all costs and expenses of litigation.

This duty to defend is generally absolute unless the insurance carrier can demonstrate that there is no possibility they will be obligated to indemnify the policyholder based on the allegations contained in the complaint, even if those allegations were, in fact, proved to be true.

For example, a complaint that contains allegations of intentional misconduct is not covered under a liability policy, thus, the insurance carrier can assert that there is no duty to defend the claim.

Settlement

An insurance carrier is obligated to the insured to exercise good faith in settling all claims made under the policy. If a settlement can be reached which is within the limits of the policy, the insurance carrier has no obligation to obtain the consent of the insured absent an express provision to that effect.

Nevertheless, as a matter of ethics, the attorney hired by the insurance carrier in connection with the claim will generally discuss the proposed settlement with the insured, including all of the facts and circumstances relating to the claim and the proposed terms of the settlement. It is also arguable that failure to do so is a breach of the attorney/client relationship since the insured is the client of the attorney hired by the insurance carrier.

If an insurance carrier fails to properly investigate the claim, and make a reasonable settlement within the policy limits where such settlement is indicated, the insurance carrier may be liable for any excess judgment over the policy limits obtained at trial.

If the verdict rendered at trial is within the policy limits, the insurance carrier does not have an obligation to appeal the verdict. However, if the insurance carrier did not make a good faith obligation to settle the claim within the policy limits, a duty to appeal a verdict awarded in excess of the policy limits may arise.

Excess Coverage

A hospital malpractice insurance policy will also generally contain a clause providing that, if there is other available coverage, such as a policy obtained by a private attending physician who is the subject of the claim, the hospital policy only covers the excess above the limits of the other policy.

Self-Insurance

A hospital that is "self-insured" chooses to retain the risk that is shifted to an insurance carrier by virtue of an insurance policy. In such a case, the hospital maintains a self-insurance fund from which defense costs and losses are paid.

CHAPTER 7:
THE HIPAA PRIVACY RULE

IN GENERAL

Information concerning an individual's medical condition is of interest to a number of entities for a variety of reasons, including insurance carriers, employers, health care providers, government agencies, and law enforcement. Technological advances have made accessing, disseminating and sharing an individual's medical records relatively easy and swift. However, without legal safeguards, there is the potential for virtually unlimited access to an individual's medical records without his or her knowledge or consent.

The danger in allowing the unauthorized dissemination of an individual's medical records is that certain entities may adversely use this information to the patient's detriment. For example, insurance carriers may refuse to issue life and health insurance policies to those individuals they deem to be at risk based on their medical history.

In addition, employers may be unwilling to employ individuals who they deem are unhealthy based on their medical records. In fact, a study by the University of Illinois found that thirty five percent (35%) of Fortune 500 companies admitted to checking medical records prior to hiring or promoting employees.

Further, law enforcement agencies may access and use an individual's medical records obtained without authorization or warrant as evidence in connection with the prosecution of a criminal matter, e.g., for identification purposes.

THE HEALTH INSURANCE PORTABILITY AND ACCOUNTABILITY ACT

In enacting the Health Insurance Portability and Accountability Act (HIPAA) Privacy Rule, Congress mandated the establishment of Federal standards for the privacy of individuals' medical records and other personal health information. For example, the Privacy Rule:

1. Gives patients more control over their health information;

2. Sets boundaries on the use and release of health records;

3. Establishes appropriate safeguards that health care providers and others must achieve to protect the privacy of health information;

4. Holds violators accountable, with civil and criminal penalties that can be imposed if they violate patients' privacy rights; and

5. Strikes a balance when public responsibility supports disclosure of some forms of data—for example, to protect public health.

The Privacy Rule also enables patients to make informed choices when seeking care and reimbursement for care based on how personal health information may be used. For example, the Privacy Rule:

1. Enables patients to find out how their information may be used, and about certain disclosures of their information that have been made;

2. Limits the release of information to the minimum reasonably needed for the purpose of the disclosure;

3. Gives patients the right to examine and obtain a copy of their own health records and request corrections; and

4. Empowers individuals to control certain uses and disclosures of their health information.

COVERED ENTITIES

As required by Congress in HIPAA, the Privacy Rule covers:

1. Health plans;

2. Health care clearinghouses; and

3. Health care providers who conduct certain financial and administrative transactions electronically. These electronic transactions are those for which standards have been adopted by the Secretary under HIPAA, such as electronic billing and fund transfers. The covered entities are bound by the privacy standards even if they contract with others to perform some of their essential functions.

COMPLIANCE

The Privacy Rule requires the average health care provider or health plan to:

1. Notify patients about their privacy rights and how their information can be used;

2. Adopt and implement privacy procedures for its practice, hospital, or plan;

3. Train employees so that they understand the privacy procedures;

4. Designate an individual to be responsible for seeing that the privacy procedures are adopted and followed; and

5. Secure patient records containing individually identifiable health information so that they are not readily available to those who do not need them.

THE HIPAA COMPLIANT AUTHORIZATION

An HIPAA compliant authorization is a detailed document that gives covered entities permission to use protected health information for specified purposes, which are generally other than treatment, payment, or health care operations, or to disclose protected health information to a third party specified by the individual.

The authorization must specify a number of elements, including;

1. A description of the protected health information to be used and disclosed;

2. The person authorized to make the use or disclosure;

3. The person to whom the covered entity may make the disclosure;

4. An expiration date; and

5. The purpose for which the information may be used or disclosed.

The Privacy Rule does not require the authorization to be notarized or witnessed.

A sample Authorization for the Release of Health Information Pursuant to HIPAA is set forth in Appendix 19.

Information to be Disclosed

Based on the signed authorization, a covered entity may use or disclose a patient's entire medical record provided the authorization describes, among other things, the information to be used or disclosed by the covered entity in a "specific and meaningful fashion." For example, an authorization would be valid if it authorized the covered entity to use or disclose an "entire medical record" or "complete patient file."

However, an authorization that authorizes the covered entity to use or disclose "all protected health information" might not be sufficiently specific. This is because protected health information encompasses a wider range of information than that which is typically understood to be included in the "medical record," and individuals are less likely to understand the extent of the information that may be defined as "protected health information."

Under the Privacy Rule, a covered entity may use or disclose protected health information pursuant to a copy of a valid and signed Authorization, including a copy that is received by facsimile or electronically transmitted.

In addition, the Privacy Rule permits a covered entity to disclose protected health information to another health care provider for treatment purposes, by fax or by other means. Covered entities must have in place reasonable and appropriate administrative, technical, and physical safeguards to protect the privacy of protected health information that is disclosed using a fax machine, e.g., placement of the fax machine in a secure location to prevent unauthorized access to the information.

Expiration of the Authorization

The Privacy Rule requires that the authorization contain either an expiration date or an expiration event that relates to the individual or the purpose of the use or disclosure. For example, an authorization may expire "one year from the date the authorization is signed," or "upon conclusion of litigation."

The authorization remains valid until its expiration date or event, unless effectively revoked in writing by the individual before that date or event.

In addition, a covered entity may disclose protected health information specified in an authorization, even if that information was created after the authorization was signed, provided that (1) the authorization encompasses the type of information that was later created; and (2) the authorization has not expired or been revoked by the individual.

Revocation of the Authorization

The Privacy Rule gives individuals the right to revoke an authorization they have given at any time. The revocation must be in writing, and is not effective until the covered entity receives it. In addition, a written revocation is not effective with respect to actions a covered entity took in reliance on a valid authorization.

In addition, the Privacy Rule requires the authorization to clearly state the individual's right to revoke, and the process for revocation must be set forth clearly on the authorization itself. In the alternative, if the covered entity creates the authorization, and its Notice of Privacy Practices contains a clear description of the revocation process, the authorization can refer to the Notice of Privacy Practices.

HEALTH CARE POWER OF ATTORNEY

If an individual has been given a health care power of attorney by the patient, the individual will have the right to access the patient's medical records to the extent permitted by the Privacy Rule.

Nevertheless, when a physician or other covered entity reasonably believes that an individual, including an unemancipated minor, has been or may be subjected to domestic violence, abuse or neglect by the personal representative, or that treating a person as an individual's personal representative could endanger the individual, the covered entity may choose not to treat that person as the individual's personal representative, if in the exercise of professional judgment, doing so would not be in the best interests of the individual.

ACCESSING YOUR MINOR CHILD'S MEDICAL RECORDS

Under the Privacy Rule, a parent has the right to obtain all of his or her child's medical records, as his or her minor child's personal representative, when such access is not inconsistent with state or other law.

There are certain circumstances when the parent would not be the minor's personal representative under the Privacy Rule, as follows:

1. The parent does not have authority to act for the child, e.g., parental rights have been terminated;

2. A state or applicable law expressly prohibits disclosure;

3. The covered entity, in the exercise of professional judgment, believes that providing such information would not be in the best interest of the individual because of a reasonable belief that the individual may be subject to abuse or neglect;

4. The minor is the one who consents to care and the consent of the parent is not required under state or other applicable law;

5. The minor obtains care at the direction of a court or a person appointed by the court; and

6. When, and to the extent that, the parent agrees that the minor and the health care provider may have a confidential relationship.

However, even in these exceptional situations, the parent may have access to the medical records of the minor related to the child's treatment when state or other applicable law requires or permits such parental access.

Parental access would be denied when state or other law prohibits such access. If state or other applicable law is silent on a parent's right of access in these cases, the licensed health care provider may exercise his or her professional judgment to the extent allowed by law to grant or deny parental access to the minor's medical information.

State Law

The Privacy Rule defers to state or other applicable law that addresses the disclosure of health information to a parent about a minor child.

If the minor child is permitted, under state law, to consent to health care without the consent of his or her parent, and does consent to such care, the provider may notify the parent when the state law explicitly requires or permits the health provider to do so.

If state law permits the minor child to consent to health care without parental consent, but is silent on parental notification, the provider would need the child's permission to notify a parent.

Age of Majority or Emancipation

When the minor child reaches the age of majority or becomes emancipated, he or she can exercise all the rights granted by the Privacy Rule with respect to all protected health information, including information obtained while the individual was an unemancipated minor.

Generally, the parent would no longer be the personal representative of his or her child once the child reaches the age of majority or becomes emancipated, and therefore, would no longer control the health information about his or her child.

ACCESSING THE MEDICAL RECORDS OF A DECEASED RELATIVE

The HIPAA Privacy Rule recognizes that a deceased relative's protected health information may be relevant to a family member's health care. The Rule provides two ways for a surviving family member to obtain the protected health information of a deceased relative.

1. Disclosure of protected health information for treatment purposes— even the treatment of another individual—does not require an authorization; thus, a covered entity may disclose a decedent's protected health information, without authorization, to the health care provider who is treating the surviving relative.

2. A covered entity must treat a deceased individual's legally authorized executor or administrator, or a person who is otherwise legally authorized to act on the behalf of the deceased individual or his estate, as a personal representative with respect to protected health information relevant to such representation. Therefore, if it is within the scope of such personal representative's authority under other law, the Rule permits the personal representative to obtain the information or provide the appropriate authorization for its disclosure.

DISCLOSURE OF PROTECTED HEALTH INFORMATION TO FAMILY AND OTHER INDIVIDUALS

Agreement of Patient

Under the Privacy Rule, a covered entity may discuss a patient's health status, treatment, or payment information with the patient's family and other individuals provided the patient agrees or, when given the opportunity, the patient does not object. The covered entity may also share relevant information with the family and other individuals if it can reasonably infer, based on professional judgment, that the patient does not object. For example:

1. A doctor may give information about a patient's mobility limitations to a friend driving the patient home from the hospital.

2. A hospital may discuss a patient's payment options with her adult daughter.

3. A doctor may instruct a patient's roommate about proper medicine dosage when she comes to pick up her friend from the hospital.

4. A physician may discuss a patient's treatment with the patient in the presence of a friend when the patient brings the friend to a medical appointment and asks if the friend can come into the treatment room.

In addition, the Privacy Rule expressly permits a covered entity to use professional judgment and experience to make reasonable inferences about the patient's best interests in allowing another person to act on behalf of the patient to pick up a filled prescription, medical supplies, X-rays, or other similar forms of protected health information.

For example, when a person comes to a pharmacy requesting to pick up a prescription on behalf of an individual he identifies by name, a pharmacist, based on professional judgment and experience with common practice, may allow the person to do so. The patient does not need to provide the pharmacist with the name of such person in advance.

Emergency or Incapacitation

Even when the patient is not present, or it is impracticable because of emergency circumstances or the patient's incapacity to ask the patient about discussing her care or payment with a family member or other person, a covered entity may share this information with the person when, in exercising professional judgment, it determines that doing so would be in the best interest of the patient. For example:

1. A surgeon may, if consistent with such professional judgment, inform a patient's spouse, who accompanied her husband to the emergency room, that the patient has suffered a heart attack, and provide periodic updates on the patient's progress and prognosis.

2. A doctor may, if consistent with such professional judgment, discuss an incapacitated patient's condition with a family member over the phone.

Disclosure for the Purposes of Notification and Identification

Under the Privacy Rule, doctor or hospital is permitted to disclose a patient's protected health information to a person or entity that can assist in notifying a patient's family member of the patient's location, health condition, or death.

The patient's written authorization is not required to make disclosures to notify, identify, or locate the patient's family members, his or her personal representatives, or other persons responsible for the patient's care.

Where the patient is present, or is otherwise available prior to the disclosure, and has capacity to make health care decisions, the covered entity may disclose protected health information for notification purposes only if the patient agrees or, when given the opportunity, does not object.

The covered entity may also make the disclosure for notification purposes if it can reasonably infer from the circumstances, based on professional judgment, that the patient does not object.

Even if the patient is not present, or it is impracticable because of emergency or incapacity to ask the patient about notifying someone, a covered entity can still disclose a patient's location, general condition, or death for notification purposes when, in exercising professional judgment, it determines that doing so would be in the best interest of the patient.

For example:

1. A doctor may share information about a patient's condition with the American Red Cross for the Red Cross to provide emergency communications services for members of the U.S. military, such as notifying service members of family illness or death, including verifying such illnesses for emergency leave requests.

2. A hospital may ask police to help locate and communicate with the family of an individual killed or injured in an accident.

3. A hospital may contact a patient's employer for information to assist in locating the patient's spouse so that he or she may be notified about the hospitalization of the patient.

PREEMPTION OF STATE LAWS

State laws that are contrary to the Privacy Rule are preempted by the Federal requirements. Contrary means that it would be impossible for a covered entity to comply with both the state and federal requirements, or that the provision of state law is an obstacle to accomplishing the full purposes and objectives of the Privacy Rule.

Nevertheless, a state law may not be preempted by the Privacy Rule if a specific exception applies, as follows:

1. A state law relates to the privacy of individually identifiable health information and is more stringent than the Privacy Rule, i.e., the state law provides greater privacy protections or privacy rights with respect to such information;

2. A state law provides for the reporting of disease or injury, child abuse, birth, or death, or for public health surveillance, investigation, or intervention; or

3. A state law requires certain health plan reporting, such as for management or financial audits. In these circumstances, a covered entity is not required to comply with a contrary provision of the Privacy Rule.

In addition, the Department of Health and Human Services (HHS) may, upon specific request from a state or other entity or person, determine that a provision of state law which is "contrary" to the Federal requirements, and which meets certain additional criteria, will not be preempted by the Federal requirements.

Thus, preemption of a contrary state law will not occur if the designated HHS official determines, in response to a request, that one of the following criteria apply:

1. The state law is necessary to prevent fraud and abuse related to the provision of or payment for health care;

2. The state law is necessary to ensure appropriate state regulation of insurance and health plans to the extent expressly authorized by statute or regulation;

3. The state law is necessary for state reporting on health care delivery or costs;

4. The state law is necessary for purposes of serving a compelling public health, safety, or welfare need; or

5. The state law has, as its principal purpose, the regulation of the manufacture, registration, distribution, dispensing, or other control of any controlled substances, or that is deemed a controlled substance by state law.

FILING A COMPLAINT

If you believe that your privacy rights have been violated, and that a covered entity is not complying with a requirement of the Privacy rule, you may file a written complaint with the Office of Civil Rights (OCR). The OCR has authority to receive and investigate complaints against covered entities related to the Privacy Rule.

Complaints to the OCR must:

1. Be filed in writing, either on paper or electronically;

2. Name the entity that is the subject of the complaint and describe the acts or omissions believed to be in violation of the applicable requirements of the Privacy Rule; and

3. Be filed within 180 days of when you knew that the act or omission complained of occurred. The OCR may extend the 180-day period if you can show "good cause."

Anyone can file written complaints with OCR by mail, fax, or email. The complaint can be submitted in any written format, but should include the following information:

1. Your name, full address, home and work telephone numbers, and email address.

2. If you are filing a complaint on someone's behalf, provide the name of the person on whose behalf you are filing.

3. The name, full address and phone of the person, agency or organization you believe violated your health information privacy rights or committed another violation of the Privacy Rule.

4. Briefly describe what happened, e.g., how, why, and when you believe your health information privacy rights were violated, or the Privacy Rule was otherwise violated.

The following information is optional:

1. Whether you need special accommodations for the OCR to communicate with you about this complaint.

2. Whether there is another individual the OCR can contact to assist in reaching you if the OCR is unable reach you.

3. Whether you have filed your complaint anywhere else.

In addition, you must sign your name and date your letter.

The OCR has ten regional offices, and each regional office covers certain states. You should send your complaint to the appropriate OCR Regional Office, based on the region where the alleged violation took place. Complaints should be sent to the attention off the appropriate OCR Regional Manager. Assistance in filing a complaint may be obtained by calling the OCR at 1-800-369-1019.

Individuals also have a right to file a complaint directly with the covered entity, and should refer to the covered entity's notice of privacy practices for more information about how to file a complaint with the covered entity.

CHAPTER 8:
NURSING HOME NEGLECT AND ABUSE

IN GENERAL

Approximately one and a half million elderly and disabled adults presently reside in nursing homes in the United States. Depending on the level of care needed by the individual, nursing homes offer varying levels of care. For example, many nursing homes are merely residential facilities that provide room and board, and general assistance with daily activities for the residents. There are no medical services available.

A higher level of care is offered in a facility known as a skilled nursing home. A skilled nursing home provides health care to its residents, who are likely in need of special medical services. A skilled nursing home also employs health care providers, such as nurses, to attend to the residents.

Unfortunately, abuse and neglect in the nursing home setting has become a widespread problem. There have been reports of serious injuries and deaths of many helpless nursing home residents, who are often left to needlessly suffer. This is due, in large part, to the lack of credentials required of nursing home employees, as well as the problem of understaffing. In addition, many nursing home employees have no training, are underpaid and overworked.

INVESTIGATE THE NURSING HOME AND STAFF

In order to reduce the possibility of any type of negligence in the nursing home setting, family members should investigate the background of the home and its staff, including the staff to resident ratio. If it is a skilled nursing home, one should also inquire into the credentials and training of the medical staff, such as the nursing staff, to determine whether they are trained in the area of the prospective resident's diagnosis.

For example, if a family member is suffering from Alzheimer's Disease, determine whether the medical staff at the nursing home has experience working with such patients. In addition, find out the ratio of nurses to residents, and the level of need required by the other residents, to ensure that there is adequate medical coverage.

Medicare/Medicaid Certification

It is important to find out whether the prospective nursing home is Medicare/Medicaid certified and whether the nursing staff and administrator are properly licensed. Medicare and Medicaid will only pay for care in a certified nursing home. To be certified, nursing homes must be in compliance with the federal requirements for long-term care as prescribed in the U.S. Code of Federal Regulations.

In addition, the nursing home must submit to an inspection survey undertaken by a state government agency. The purpose of the survey process is to assess whether the quality of care, as intended by the law and regulations, and as needed by the resident, is actually being provided in nursing homes.

In order to remain certified, nursing homes must be in substantial compliance with the Medicaid and Medicare care requirements as well as state law. If a nursing home is found to be out of compliance, federal law sets forth enforcement options such as denial of payment for new admissions, civil money penalties, revocation of Medicaid and Medicare certifications, transfer of residents and the imposition of temporary management. If the nursing home fails to meet a federal regulation, a deficiency is issued.

A comparison of nursing homes in one's area can be made by going to the "Nursing Home Compare" page of the Medicare website (www.medicare.gov). At this website, one can review the state inspection reports of the nursing homes in the area, as well as resident characteristics and staffing levels. The service has information about nursing homes in all 50 States, the District of Columbia, and some U.S. Territories.

The quality information contained on the website includes:

1. The percentage of residents with loss of ability in basic daily tasks since their need for help was last assessed;

2. The percentage of residents with pressure sores, commonly referred to as bedsores;

3. The percentage of residents with bad or moderate enduring pain;

4. The percentage of residents with infections, including pneumonia, wound infections, urinary tract or a bladder infection;

5. The percentage of residents in physical restraints;

6. The percentage of short-stay residents—i.e., residents who stay for less than 90 days;

7. The percentage of short-stay residents with pain; and

8. The percentage of short-stay residents with delirium.

Long-Term Care Ombudsman

Another way of determining quality of care is by contacting the state office of Long-Term Care Ombudsman. The Ombudsman program is a very good source of general information about nursing homes. Ombudsmen visit nursing homes and speak with residents throughout the year to make sure residents' rights are protected. They also work to solve any problems a resident may have with their nursing home care, including quality of care and financial issues.

The Ombudsman program may be able to share information concerning the number and type of complaints they have received about a particular nursing home, and how those problems were resolved.

The Joint Commission

As set forth in Chapter 1, "Hospital Organization," the Joint Commission is dedicated to improving the safety and quality of care provided to the public through their health care organization accreditation program, which includes nursing homes and other long-term care facilities. Joint Commission accreditation is recognized nationwide as a symbol of quality that indicates an organization meets certain performance standards. To earn and maintain accreditation, an organization must undergo an on-site survey by a Joint Commission survey team at least every three years.

The Joint Commission also publishes "Quality Check"—a comprehensive internet guide to accredited organizations. Quality Check provides a searchable database of accredited health care organizations and programs throughout the United States and includes each organization's name, address, telephone number, accreditation decision, accreditation date, and current accreditation status and effective date.

In addition, for more in-depth quality information, consumers can check the individual performance reports available for many accredited organizations. Performance reports provide detailed information about an organization's performance and how it compares to similar organizations.

VISIT THE NURSING HOME

Before selecting a nursing home, it is important to visit the facility. A visit gives you the chance to see and speak with the residents and staff, and view the facility and accommodations. When you visit the nursing home, it is important to bring a checklist so that you do not forget to ask any important questions. This checklist has questions about basic information, resident appearance, nursing home living spaces, staff, residents' rooms, hallways, stairs, lounges, bathrooms, menus and food, activities, and safety and care.

A nursing home checklist prepared by the Centers for Medicare and Medicaid Services is set forth in Appendix 20.

Also ask for a copy of the nursing home's inspection report as discussed above. The inspection report will tell you how well the nursing home meets federal health and safety requirements. The nursing home is required to maintain and make available the results of the most recent survey undertaken of the facility by federal or state surveyors.

You should also make arrangements to revisit the nursing home on another weekday and/or weekend, and at a different time of day to compare the atmosphere and activities, and meet additional members of the staff who may not have been on duty during your first visit.

Nursing homes also hold "council" meetings among the staff, residents and family members. Ask for permission to attend one of the council meetings so you can assess the opinion of the current residents and family members.

If you are uncomfortable about anything you see, or anyone you meet, at a particular nursing home, you may want to trust your instincts and choose another nursing home. If, however, it appears that the facility is clean and well-kept, the residents seem comfortable and treated well, and the staff is friendly and available, that can help in making a good decision.

MONITOR THE NURSING HOME

The best way to monitor how your loved one is being treated is to make yourself visible. Make frequent visits to the facility to speak with the staff. Show up at different times of the day, and on different days, so that the staff is not prepared for your visit. Join the family council and attend the meetings. Demonstrate your knowledge of the applicable state and federal laws and regulations.

If your family member is in ill health and needs specialized attention, it is even more crucial that you become involved, and be alert to potential problems. If your family member needs assistance in feeding and drinking, it is especially important to make sure these needs are being taken care of because dehydration and malnutrition are serious problems in nursing homes, and can lead to life-threatening diseases and death.

Take time to visit the nursing home around mealtime. Make sure that the food is nutritious, balanced and served warm, and that drinks are readily available. If your family member is unable to self-feed, make sure that staff members are taking their time in feeding him or her. This take patience.

During your visits, watch for the following signs of neglect:

1. Lack of assistance with feeding those residents who cannot feed themselves.

2. Lack of respect for the residents, such as harsh or disrespectful language.

3. Lack of privacy, e.g., residents should be clothed when in the common areas, and should be able to expect privacy when they are in their own rooms or in the bathroom.

4. Strong offensive odors, such as the smell of urine or feces, may indicate that there are not people on staff to attend to all of the resident's personal needs, or to maintain the cleanliness of the nursing home.

5. The use of restraints is humiliating, dangerous if not properly monitored, and may indicate that the nursing home is not able to attend to the safety of all of the residents in a more respectful manner.

6. Many unanswered call bells may be another indication that there are not enough staff members to attend to the needs of the residents.

THE PROBLEM OF UNDERSTAFFING

Understaffing is a serious problem in nursing homes that can lead to the neglect and abuse of nursing home residents. According to studies, understaffing is directly linked to poor nursing home care, which is in turn linked to the increased hospitalization of nursing home residents.

More than one-half of American nursing homes are below the suggested minimum staffing level for nurse's aides, and more than one-third of nursing homes fell below the suggested minimum staffing level for registered nurses. Of total licensed staff, nearly one-fourth of all nursing homes routinely fall below the suggested minimum staffing level. State and federal laws require that nursing homes receiving federal funds must maintain a sufficient number of employees to care for the residents.

Therefore, it is important to keep track of the staff to resident ratio. If there is a low staff to resident ratio, it is impossible to make sure all of the residents' needs are properly being met. You should visit as much as possible to make sure your loved one is eating and drinking properly, and that their personal hygiene is properly maintained, to avoid serious illness.

LEGAL RIGHTS OF NURSING HOME RESIDENTS

State and federal laws provide certain rights and protections to nursing home residents. It is important for the resident and his or her family members to familiarize themselves with the federal and state laws concerning the nursing home resident's rights. The nursing home is required to post these rights in the facility, and provide the resident with a written description of these legal rights.

Nursing homes that receive federal funding are required to comply with the federal laws that guarantee a high level of care to nursing home residents. In addition to federal laws regulating the quality of care in nursing homes, states have enacted laws as well. State laws may vary, therefore, the reader is advised to check the law of his or her own jurisdiction. The rights under state law, however, must compare with, or exceed, the rights provided under federal laws. In fact, some states have adopted laws that are tougher than the federal laws.

Any violation of a resident's rights should be reported to the nursing home, following the established grievance procedures. If the problem is not addressed and corrected, the violation should be reported to the local long-term care ombudsman.

Following is a list of the rights of nursing home residents:

1. The Right to be Free from Discrimination—Nursing homes do not have to accept all applicants, but they must comply with Civil Rights laws that do not allow discrimination based on race, color, national origin, disability, age, or religion under certain conditions.

2. The Right to be Treated Respectfully—A nursing home resident has the right to be treated with dignity and respect. The resident has

the right to make their own schedule, including when they sleep, when they wake, and when they eat. They can choose which activities they want to engage in, and which they want to avoid. The only exception is that the resident's choice must conform to their plan of care.

3. The Right to be Free from Abuse and Neglect—A nursing home resident has the right to be free from verbal, sexual, physical, and mental abuse, and involuntary seclusion by anyone, including but not limited to nursing home staff, other residents, consultants, volunteers, staff from other agencies, family members or legal guardians, friends, or other individuals.

4. The Right to be Free From Restraints—It is against the law for a nursing home to use physical or chemical restraints, unless it is necessary to treat the resident's medical symptoms, or if the resident is at risk of harming oneself or another. A physical restraint prevents freedom of movement or normal access to one's own body. A chemical restraint is a drug used to limit freedom of movement and is not needed to treat the person's medical symptoms. Restraints may not be used to punish the resident, nor can a restraint be used for the convenience of nursing home staff.

5. The Right to Receive Information on Services and Fees—A nursing home resident must be informed, in writing, about services and fees before they move into the nursing home. In addition, the nursing home cannot require a minimum entrance fee.

6. The Right to Manage Their Money—A nursing home resident has the right to manage their own money or to choose someone they trust to manage their money. If the resident wants the nursing home to manage their personal funds, they must sign a written statement giving the nursing home permission to do so. The nursing home must protect the resident's funds from loss by buying a bond or some other type of protection method. In addition, the nursing home must provide the resident with access to their financial records, bank account, and cash reserve.

7. The Right to Privacy—A nursing home resident has the right to privacy. This includes the right to make telephone calls in private. In addition, the nursing home resident is entitled to keep his or her own personal property. Nevertheless, the nursing home is obligated to protect the resident's property from theft, e.g., by providing locked cabinets in the rooms. Nursing home staff is not permitted to open a resident's mail unless authorized by the resident.

8. The Right to Joint Living Space for Married Couple—If married residents are living in the same nursing home, they are entitled to share a room.

9. The Right to be Informed About Their Medical Care—A nursing home resident has the right to be informed about his or her medical condition and any medications they are given. A resident also has the right to refuse any medication or treatment. The resident has the right to take part in developing his or her care plan, and must be given access to his or her medical records upon request. In addition, a resident has the right to see his or her own doctor.

10. The Right to Visitors—A nursing home resident has the right to spend private time with visitors, including those providing medical or legal services, at any reasonable hour. In addition, the nursing home must permit family members to visit the resident at any time. The resident also has the right to refuse to see any visitor.

11. The Right to Necessary Social Services—A nursing home resident has the right to necessary social services, including but not limited to counseling, legal assistance, and discharge coordination.

12. The Right to File Grievances—A nursing home resident has the right to complain without fear of reprisal. The nursing home is obligated to promptly address and resolve the resident's complaint.

NURSING HOME NEGLECT

Nursing home neglect involves the failure to provide reasonable care for a person. Some of the most common injuries resulting from nursing home negligence are discussed below.

Malnutrition and Dehydration

Malnutrition and dehydration may occur if the nursing home staff fails to provide adequate food and/or water to the resident. Thus, it is crucial that nursing homes recognize the increased risk of malnutrition and dehydration that elderly people face, and take adequate preventive measures.

Malnutrition results from the lack of a proper diet, including essential vitamins and nutrients. It can be a serious, life-threatening condition for an elderly person. Dehydration results from inadequate hydration— i.e., the individual's loss of fluids exceeds his or her intake of fluids. Dehydration can also lead to a variety of serious health problems and death.

Unfortunately, these conditions often occur because of nursing home negligence. For example, if a nursing home is understaffed, there is not enough manpower or time to make sure all of the residents are properly fed and hydrated. In addition, the lack of training of nursing home staff makes it unlikely that they would be able to recognize the signs of malnutrition or dehydration until the condition has progressed to a dangerous level.

Pressure Sores

Pressure sores, more commonly known as bedsores, are painful skin ulcers that result from prolonged pressure on a body part that has a thin covering of skin over bone, such as the tailbone, shoulders, elbows, etc. In a nursing home setting, bedsores are often caused by the presence of moisture due to wet sheets or clothing, or the failure of the staff to regularly reposition a bedridden patient. Bedsores may also be caused by dehydration and malnutrition. Bedsores are extremely painful and a serious health problem. If the ulcers become too deep or infected, they can lead to death. Nevertheless, this condition can be cured and prevented with adequate care.

The law requires a nursing home to ensure that a resident does not develop bedsores to the extent the condition is avoidable. If the development of bedsores is avoidable, and is due to the nursing home's lack of care, the nursing home may be liable for negligence. If your loved one has developed bedsores, and you are dissatisfied with the way the nursing home is treating the condition, the resident should be taken to a hospital emergency room for evaluation and treatment.

In order to determine whether the condition was preventable, one must consider a number of factors concerning the care given, including: (i) whether an immobile resident was regularly repositioned; (ii) whether care was taken to change wet sheets and clothing; (iii) the condition of the resident's skin upon admission; (iv) the severity of the bedsores; (v) whether a health care professional was called to examine the resident's condition; and (vi) whether the resident had any underlying medical problems that contributed to the condition.

Falls

Many nursing home injuries result from falls. Many of these falls lead to serious injuries, such as fractures, and even death. The law requires a nursing home to take safety precautions to prevent falls. Although some falls are purely accidental, and nobody is to blame, some falls are caused entirely by the negligence of the nursing home.

Such falls may be caused by: (i) inadequate supervision; (ii) dimly lit passageways; (iii) wet floors; (iv) cluttered hallways; (v) lack of bedrails or handrails; (vi) employees who are improperly trained in lifting residents; and (vii) improper bed heights; etc.

When a resident is admitted, his or her risk of falling should be assessed to determine whether the resident needs any special device to prevent a fall, such as a walker. If a nursing home was put on notice that a resident was at risk for falling, and they failed to take preventive measures, or if they created the unsafe condition that caused the fall, the nursing home may be liable for negligence.

Depending on the severity of the injury, a lawsuit may be initiated to recover for the resident's damages, including his or her pain and suffering as a result of the fall.

Wandering and Elopement

Wandering is a common problem among nursing home residents who are cognitively impaired. Such persons are found walking around the nursing home aimlessly, without any awareness of their surroundings. This can lead to serious injury. Elopement is a type of wandering, however, it refers to the ability of the resident to leave the facility undetected and unsupervised.

The law requires that a nursing home provide adequate supervision to prevent incidents of wandering and elopement. When a person is admitted to the nursing home, his or her risk of wandering or elopement must be evaluated and included in the resident's plan of care. Residents who are at high risk for wandering and elopement are those who suffer from dementia, Alzheimer's disease, and those who are on medications that may cause confusion.

A nursing home may be liable for negligence if it is aware of a resident's tendency for wandering or elopement, it fails to take adequate security measures to prevent this behavior, and the resident is injured as a result.

Inadequate security measures may include, but are not limited to: (i) understaffing; (ii) failure to properly train employees on wandering and elopement behaviors; (iii) the absence of alarm systems designed to prevent wandering and/or elopement; and (iv) the failure of employees to properly supervise at risk residents.

NURSING HOME ABUSE

While neglect involves the failure to provide reasonable care for a person, abuse refers to intentionally causing pain or injury to another. Nursing home abuse may take many forms, and includes: (i) physical abuse, such as assault and battery; (ii) sexual assault and battery, including sexual molestation and rape; (iii) mental and emotional abuse; (iv) verbal abuse and intimidation; (v) the deprivation of food or water for prolonged periods of time; (vi) unreasonable and prolonged physical restraints; (vii) unreasonable seclusion; and (viii) corporal punishment.

Federal and state laws provide that a resident in a nursing home has the right to be free from physical, sexual, and mental abuse, as well as involuntary seclusion. In addition, there are federal and state regulations aimed at preventing the employment of individuals who have been convicted of abuse, neglect or maltreatment in a health care setting.

There are a number of agencies that should be contacted if a nursing home resident is subjected to abuse, including: (i) the local law enforcement officials; (ii) the state office of aging; (iii) the state long-term care ombudsman; (iv) the state licensing and certification agency; and (v) the state's adult protective services office.

Some of the most common injuries resulting from nursing home negligence are discussed below.

Physical Abuse

Physical abuse is the intentional use of physical force upon an individual that is likely to result in bodily injury or pain. Physical abuse occurs when a staff member or co-resident physically assaults the resident. This may include but is not limited to hitting, punching, shoving, slapping, kicking, burning, shaking, or force-feeding the resident.

Indications that a nursing home resident may be the victim of physical abuse include: (i) unexplained black eyes; (ii) sprains; (iii) fractures; (iv) cuts and bruises; (v) internal bleeding; and (vi) hair loss.

In addition, if a family member is denied access to the resident, this should raise a warning signal that something may be wrong. In such a case, carefully examine the resident and watch for any unusual change in the resident's behavior, such as anxiety, fear or stress, particularly if there is a strong reaction to certain nursing home employees or co-residents.

Be aware that if the resident does not admit being victimized, he or she may fear retaliation from the abusive staff member. It may take some time to convince the victim that they do not have anything to fear. Once the abuse has been confirmed, immediately contact local law enforcement authorities and obtain medical help.

If you suspect that your loved one has been the victim of physical abuse, and there is evidence of possible abuse, but he or she will not admit it, or is unable to communicate effectively, law enforcement should still be called and the person should be taken for medical evaluation. If you are not sure whether abuse has occurred, you should still confidentially convey your suspicions to the nursing home administrator, and ask that the situation be monitored.

Sexual Abuse

Sexual abuse generally involves any type of nonconsensual sexual contact, including improper touching and forced sexual acts, such as rape and sodomy. Sadly, elderly nursing home residents fall victim to sexual abuse because of their fragility and inability to defend themselves. In addition, many nursing home residents are unable to effectively communicate, making them easy prey for sexual predators, including staff members and co-residents.

Indications that a nursing home resident may be the victim of sexual abuse include: (i) unexplained bruising in the genital area, buttocks or breasts; (ii) difficulty walking or sitting; (iii) vaginal and/or anal bleeding; (iv) genital infections, irritation or injury; (v) sexually transmitted diseases; and (vi) torn or bloody undergarments.

Again, carefully examine the resident and watch for any unusual change in the resident's behavior, such as anxiety, fear or stress, particularly if there is a strong reaction to certain nursing home employees or co-residents.

As with suspected physical abuse described above, if there are indications of sexual abuse, law enforcement authorities must be notified and the resident must be taken for medical evaluation and treatment, whether or not the resident admits that sexual abuse has taken place.

Mental Abuse

Mental abuse involves the intentional infliction of emotional distress, fear and anguish through the use of verbal and/or nonverbal actions. Under the law, a nursing home resident has the right to be treated with dignity and respect, which includes the right to be free from mental and emotional abuse.

Verbal abuse by nursing home employees is a common problem in nursing homes, and may occur when a staff member ridicules, harasses, threatens, curses, berates and/or ignores a resident. Verbal abuse may be directed at an individual resident or generally expressed in front of a group of residents, in order to degrade and demoralize them.

Verbal threats are generally directed at a specific resident. For example, the resident may be threatened with physical harm or some type of deprivation if they don't finish their food.

Residents who are subjected to emotional or verbal abuse are often afraid to speak out, or ask for items of necessity, for fear of being ridiculed. This can lead to serious consequences. For example, a resident may be afraid to bring a physical complaint to the attention of the staff, which could lead to serious illness, or they may fear asking for a glass of water because they do not want to face verbal abuse, which could in turn lead to dehydration.

Financial Abuse

Financial abuse occurs when a staff member deliberately steals, misplaces, or misuses a resident's belongings without consent, such as the resident's money, jewelry, clothing or other personal property.

Nursing Home Liability for Abuse

Nursing homes have a duty to thoroughly investigate the background of the employees it hires. In addition, if the investigation reveals that an applicant has criminal convictions that would indicate their unsuitability for working in the nursing home setting, including convictions for crimes such as child abuse or sexual assault, the nursing home has an obligation to report that individual.

When abuse occurs, the nursing home itself may be liable for the conduct of the offending staff member if:

1. The nursing home failed to conduct an adequate background investigation that would have revealed a staff member's propensity for violence or sexual assault;

2. The nursing home was understaffed and failed to employ a sufficient number of employees to supervise the staff and residents;

3. The nursing home failed to properly train its employees concerning physical, sexual and mental abuse;

4. The nursing home failed to properly supervise its employees; or

5. The nursing home continued to employ a person who exhibited signs of aggression or improper sexual tendencies towards residents.

RESOLVING NEGLECT AND ABUSE PROBLEMS

If it appears that a nursing home resident is not getting the care they are entitled to, and have suffered neglect or abuse, there are many steps a resident and/or his family members can take to resolve the problem.

The remedy one chooses to pursue depends, in large part, on the severity of the problem. Minor problems may be resolved informally. More serious problems may require law enforcement intervention or litigation.

In any event, it is important to keep a journal which sets forth all of your grievances concerning the quality of care at the nursing home. Take notes of all details, including names, dates, witnesses, conversations, etc. If you are able to take photographs, preferably without the knowledge of the nursing home staff, this will assist in creating a record for future use should it become necessary.

Meet with the Staff

For relatively minor grievances, or concerns about an isolated incident, the first step may be to have a meeting with the nursing home staff. A friendly discussion often helps to keep a minor problem from developing into a more serious situation.

Meet with the Family Council

In Medicare and Medicaid certified nursing homes, families have a right to form family councils and meet privately in the nursing home. If there is no existing family council, you may organize a council to address nursing home concerns.

If a number of families get together and present their complaints to the nursing home administrator, there is a better chance those concerns will be addressed. In addition, the family council can join with the resident council for even greater strength.

Contact Nursing Home Advocacy Groups

If you are unable to resolve the problems within the nursing home setting, you may have to contact a nursing home advocacy group. These organizations provide information to residents and their family members who have complaints about the care the resident is receiving in a nursing home.

Advocacy groups often lobby for stronger legislation to protect the rights of nursing home residents. Information about advocacy groups in your area may be obtained by contacting your state's agency on aging or one of the national organizations for the elderly.

As discussed above, the Long-Term Care Ombudsman are strong advocates for nursing home residents. The Ombudsman investigate individual complaints of nursing home neglect and abuse, and are often able to resolve minor problems that occur between the nursing home and the resident.

If the Ombudsman are unable to resolve the problem, or if the allegations are particularly grievous, they will refer the case to a higher authority, such as the state licensing agency.

File a Complaint with the State Licensing Agencies

A complaint can be filed with the state licensing and certification agency responsible for determining whether a particular nursing home has met both the state licensing requirements and any federal regulations concerning quality of care standards. Violations can be brought to the attention of the agency, which will undertake a complaint investigation.

The state is required to investigate all complaints in a timely manner. However, if it is alleged that a dangerous condition exists in the nursing home, which is putting the residents at risk of immediate injury, the agency is required to investigate within two days of receiving the complaint.

You can request that the complaint remain confidential, however, the facility is often able to discover the name of the complainant at some point in the investigation. Making a complaint while the resident is still in the nursing home also raises concerns about retaliation.

The state can take a range of actions against a nursing home that has violated the law including: (i) ordering the nursing home to comply with the law and correct the violations; (ii) assessing a fine or suspending the facility's license to operate; (iii) appointing a temporary administrator in the facility to oversee compliance.

In serious situations, the state can stop federal Medicare and Medicaid funding to the nursing home. Insofar as most nursing homes rely on the federal Medicare and Medicaid program for most, if not all of their business, this can effectively close down a particularly substandard nursing home.

File a Complaint with the Health Care Financing Administration

The Health Care Financing Administration (HCFA) is the federal program that oversees the state inspection agencies. If the state agency does not resolve the complaint in a timely manner, a complaint may be filed with the HCFA.

The complaint should describe the problem, including dates, names, and witnesses. The length of time the condition has existed should also be stated. The complaint should also state whether the problem is an emergency or is placing the resident in immediate danger of injury. In addition, outline the steps you have taken to try and resolve the complaint.

Contact Legal Services for the Elderly

There are a number of nonprofit legal services that will provide free legal advice and representation to a nursing home resident regarding violations of the resident's rights under the law.

Although these nonprofit legal services do not represent individuals in personal injury lawsuits against a nursing home, their involvement in the grievance process may go a long way in resolving the problem. Nursing homes do not want to be under the scrutiny of such an organization and possibly face legal action for violations of the law. Residents who want to pursue individual personal injury actions must hire a private attorney, as set forth below.

Pursue Litigation

If the resident has suffered a serious injury resulting from the nursing home's neglect or abuse, it may be necessary to bring a private lawsuit against the facility. Although this may be time-consuming and expensive, it forces the nursing home to address the problem. The type of lawsuit that must be initiated depends on the type of injury sustained.

When a lawyer is hired on behalf of the resident, he or she will investigate the complaint, evaluate the injury and make a determination as to who is responsible. Successful litigation may result in a monetary award to compensate the resident for his or her medical expenses, and pain and suffering. In cases of gross negligence, or intentional acts, the resident may be entitled to recovery punitive damages as well.Punitive damages are assessed as a way of punishing the wrongful party.

APPENDIX 1:
DIRECTORY OF STATE LICENSING
AGENCIES FOR MEDICAL FACILITIES

STATE	NAME	DEPARTMENT	ADDRESS	TELEPHONE
Alabama	Alabama Department of Public Health	Health Facility Licensure and Certification	State Office Building Montgomery, Alabama 36130	205-832-3253
Alaska	Department of Health and Social Services	Division of Public Health	Pouch H-06 Juneau, Alaska 99811	907-465-3090
Arizona	Department of Health	Health Facility Licensure and Certification	1740 West Adams Street, Phoenix, Arizona 85007	602-255-1118
Arkansas	Department of Health	Health Facility Services	4815 West Markham Street Little Rock, Arkansas 72201	501-661-2201
California	Department of Health Services	Health Facilities Licensure and Certification	744 P Street, Sacramento, California 95814	916-445-3281
Colorado	Department of Health	Health Facility Licensure and Certification	4210 East Eleventh Avenue Denver, Colorado 80220	303-320-8333
Connecticut	Department of Health Services	Hospital and Medical Care Services	79 Elm Street Hartford, Connecticut 06115	203-566-3985

STATE	NAME	DEPARTMENT	ADDRESS	TELEPHONE
Delaware	Department of Health and Social Services	Health Facility Licensure and Certification	Jesse S. Cooper Memorial Building Dover, Delaware 19901	302-995-6674
District of Columbia	Department of Human Services	Health Facility Licensure and Certification	1875 Connecticut Avenue N.W., Washington, DC 20009	202-727-2009
Florida	Department of Health and Rehabilitative Services	Health Facility Licensure and Certification	1323 Winewood Boulevard, Tallahassee, Florida 32301	904-359-6022
Georgia	Department of Human Resources	Licensing and Certification	Atlanta, Georgia 30334	404-894-5144
Hawaii	Department of Health	Health Facility Licensure and Certification	Kinau Hale, P.O. Box 3378 Honolulu, Hawaii 96801	808-548-6510
Idaho	Department of Health and Welfare, Division of Health	Health Facility Licensure and Certification	Statehouse Mail Boise, Idaho 83720	208-334-4172
Illinois	Department of Public Health	Division of Health Facility Standards	525 West Jefferson Springfield, Illinois 62761	217-782-7412
Indiana	Indiana State Board of Health	Health Facility Licensure and Certification	1330 West Michigan Street P.O. Box 1964 Indianapolis, Indiana 46206	317-633-8442
Iowa	Department of Health	Health Facility Licensure and Certification	Lucas State Office Building Des Moines, Iowa 50319	515-281-4125
Kansas	Department of Health and Environment	Health Facility Licensure and Certification	Forbes Field, Topeka, Kansas 66620	913-862-9360

STATE	NAME	DEPARTMENT	ADDRESS	TELEPHONE
Kentucky	Department of Human Resources	Ombudsman	275 Main Street, Frankfort, Kentucky 406217	502-564-5497
Louisiana	Department of Health and Human Resources	Office of Licensing and Regulations	P.O. Box 60630, New Orleans, Louisiana 70160	504-342-6721
Maine	Department of Human Services	Health Facility Licensure and Certification	Augusta, Maine 04333	207-289-2606
Maryland	Department of Health and Mental Hygiene	Licensing and Certification	201 West Preston Street Baltimore, Maryland 21201	301-383-2517
Massa-chusetts	Office of Human Services	Health Facilities	600 Washington Street, Boston, Massachusetts 02111	617-727-6240
Michigan	Department of Public Health	Health Facility Licensing and Certification	3500 North Logan Street Lansing, Michigan 48909	517-373-0900
Minnesota	Department of Health	Health Facility Licensure and Certification	717 Delaware Street S.E. Minneapolis, Minnesota 55440	612-296-5420
Mississippi	Health Care Commission	Health Facility Licensing and Certification	2688 Insurance Center Drive Jackson, Mississippi 39201	601-981-6880
Missouri	Missouri Division of Health	Hospital Licensure and Certification	Broadway State Office Building, P.O. Box 570, Jefferson City, Missouri 65101	314-751-2713
Montana	Department of Health and Environmental Sciences	Health Facility Licensure and Certification	Cogswell Building Helena, Montana 59620	406-449-2037

STATE	NAME	DEPARTMENT	ADDRESS	TELEPHONE
Nebraska	Department of Health	Health Facility Licensure and Certification	301 Centennial Mall South Lincoln, Nebraska 68509	402-471-2105
Nevada	Department of Human Resources	Health Facility Licensure and Certification	505 East King Street Capitol Complex Carson City, Nevada 89710	702-884-4475
New Hampshire	Division of Public Health Services	Health Facility Licensure and Certification	Health and Welfare Building Hazen Drive Concord, New Hampshire 03301	603-271-4592
New Jersey	Department of Health	Health Facility Licensure and Certification	CN 360 John Fitch Plaza, Trenton, New Jersey 08625	609-292-5764
New Mexico	Health and Environment Department	Bureau of Health Facilities	P.O. Box 968, Santa Fe, New Mexico 87504	505-827-2745
New York	Department of Health, Bureau of Project Management	Division of Health Facility Planning	Corning Tower Suite 9-300, Empire State Plaza, Albany, New York 12237	518-473-4119
North Carolina	Department of Human Resources, Division of Health Services	Health Facility Licensure and Certification	P.O. Box 2091, Raleigh, North Carolina 27602	919-733-2342
North Dakota	State Department of Health	Health Facility Licensure and Certification	State Capitol, Bismarck, North Dakota 58505	701-224-2352
Ohio	Department of Health	Health Facility Licensure and Certification	P.O. Box 118, Columbus, Ohio 43216	614-466-7857
Oklahoma	State Department of Health	Health Facilities Service	P.O. Box 53551, Oklahoma City, Oklahoma 73152	405-271-5114

STATE	NAME	DEPARTMENT	ADDRESS	TELEPHONE
Oregon	Department of Human Resources	Health Facility Licensure and Certification	P.O. Box 231, Portland, Oregon 97207	503-229-5686
Pennsylvania	Department of Health	Hospital Licensing	P.O. Box 90, Harrisburg, Pennsylvania 17120	717-783-8980
Rhode Island	Department of Health Facility Regulation	Health Facility Regulation	75 Davis Street, Providence, Rhode Island 02908	401-277-2566
South Carolina	Department of Health and Environmental Control	Health Facility Licensing and Certification	2600 Bull Street Columbia, South Carolina 29201	803-758-4567
South Dakota	Department of Health	Health Facility Licensure and Certification	Joe Foss Building Pierre, South Dakota 57501	605-773-3364
Tennessee	Department of Public Health	Health Facility Licensure and Certification	Cordell Hull Building, Nashville, Tennessee 37219	615-741-6379
Texas	Department of Health	Bureau of Licensing and Certification	1100 West 49th Street Austin, Texas 78756	512-458-7538
Utah	Utah Department of Health	Health Facility Licensure and Certification	150 West North Temple P.O. Box 2500 Salt Lake City, Utah 84110	801-533-7016
Vermont	Department of Health	Health Facility Licensure and Certification	60 Main Street Burlington, Vermont 05401	802-862-5701
Virginia	State Health Department	Health Facility Licensing and Certification	109 Governor Street Richmond, Virginia 23219	804-786-2081
Washington	Department of Social and Health Services	Health Facility Licensure and Certification	Mail Stop LJ-18 Olympia, Washington 98504	206-753-5851

STATE	NAME	DEPARTMENT	ADDRESS	TELEPHONE
West Virginia	Department of Health	Health Facilities Evaluation	State Capitol Complex Charleston, West Virginia 25305	304-348-0530
Wisconsin	Division of Health	Health Facility Licensing and Certification	P.O. Box 309 Madison, Wisconsin 53701	608-266-2055
Wyoming	Health and Medical Services	Health Facility Licensure and Certification	Hathaway Building Cheyenne, Wyoming 82002	307-777-7121

APPENDIX 2:
DIRECTORY OF STATE PHYSICIAN
LICENSING BUREAUS

STATE	NAME	ADDRESS	TELEPHONE
Alabama	Alabama State Board of Medical Examiners	P.O. Box 946 Montgomery, Alabama 36102	205-832-6890
Alaska	Alaska Board of Medical Examiners	Pouch DJuneau, Alaska 99811	907-465-2541
Arizona	Arizona State Board of Medical Examiners	5060 North Nineteenth Avenue, Suite 300 Phoenix, Arizona 85015	602-255-3751
Arkansas	Arkansas State Medical Board	P.O. Box 102, Harrisburg, Arkansas 72432	501-578-2677
California	California Board of Medical Quality Assurance	1340 Howe Avenue Sacramento, California 95825	916-920-6411
Colorado	Colorado Board of Medical Examiners	132 State Services Building 1525 Sherman Street Denver, Colorado	303-866-2468
Connecticut	Connecticut Medical Examining Board	79 Elm StreetHartford, Connecticut 06115	203-566-5630
Delaware	Delaware Board of Medical Practice	Margaret O'Neill Building P.O. Box 1401 Dover, Delaware 19901	302-763-4753

STATE	NAME	ADDRESS	TELEPHONE
District of Columbia	District of Columbia Commission on Licensure to Practice the Healing Art	605 G Street N.W., Washington, DC 20001	202-727-5365
Florida	Florida Board of Medical Examiners	130 North Monroe Street Tallahassee, Florida 32301	904-488-0595
Georgia	Georgia Composite Board of Medical Examiners	166 Pryor Street, Southwest Atlanta, Georgia 30303	404-656-7067
Hawaii	Hawaii Board of Medical Examiners	P.O. Box 3469, Honolulu, Hawaii 96801	808-548-4100
Idaho	Idaho State Board of Medicine	700 West State Street, Boise, Idaho 83720	208-334-2822
Illinois	Professional Regulation	106 West Randolph, Chicago, Illinois 60601	312-917-4500
Indiana	Medical Licensing Board of Indiana	One American Square, Suite 1020, P.O. Box 82067 Indianapolis, Indiana 46282	317-232-2960
Iowa	Iowa State Board of Medical Examiners	State Capitol Complex, Executive Hills West Des Moines, Iowa 50319	515-281-5171
Kansas	Kansas State Board of Healing Arts	503 Kansas Avenue, Suite 500 Topeka, Kansas 66534	913-296-7413
Kentucky	Kentucky State Board of Medical Licensure	3532 Ephraim Drive, Louisville, Kentucky 40205	502-456-2220
Louisiana	Louisiana State Board of Medical Examiners	830 Union Street, Suite 100, New Orleans, Louisiana 70112	504-524-6763
Maine	Maine State Board of Registration in Medicine	RFD #3, Box 461, Waterville, Maine 04901	207-873-2184
Maryland	Maryland Board of Medical Examiners	201 West Preston Street, Baltimore, Maryland 21201	301-383-2020

STATE	NAME	ADDRESS	TELEPHONE
Massachusetts	Massachusetts Board of Registration in Medicine	Room 1511, Leverett Saltonstall Building, 100 Cambridge Street, Boston, Massachusetts 02202	617-727-9446
Michigan	Michigan Board of Medicine	905 Southland, P.O. Box 30018, Lansing, Michigan 48909	517-373-0680
Minnesota	Minnesota State Board of Medical Examiners	717 Delaware Street S.E., Suite 352, Minneapolis, Minnesota 55414	612-296-5534
Mississippi	Mississippi State Board of Medical Licensure	P.O. Box 1700, Jackson, Mississippi 39205	601-354-6645
Missouri	Missouri State Board of Registration for the Healing Arts	P.O. Box 4, Jefferson City, Missouri 65102	314-751-2334
Montana	Montana State Board of Medical Examiners	1424 9th Avenue, Helena, Montana 59620	406-449-3737
Nebraska	Nebraska Bureau of Examining Boards	P.O. Box 95007, Lincoln, Nebraska 68509	402-471-2115
Nevada	Nevada State Board of Medical Examiners	P.O. Box 7238, Reno, Nevada 89510	702-329-2559
New Hampshire	New Hampshire Board of Registration in Medicine	Health and Welfare Building, Hazen Drive, Concord, New Hampshire 03301	603-271-4502
New Jersey	New Jersey State Board of Medical Examiners	28 West State Street, Room 914,Trenton, New Jersey 08608	609-292-4843
New Mexico	New Mexico State Board of Medical Examiners	227 E. Palace Avenue, Santa Fe, New Mexico 87501	505-827-2215
New York	New York Department of Health, Office of Professional Medical Conduct	Empire State Plaza, Tower Building, Albany, New York 12237	518-474-8537

STATE	NAME	ADDRESS	TELEPHONE
North Carolina	North Carolina State Board of Medical Examiners	222 North Person Street, Suite 214 Raleigh, North Carolina 27601	919-833-5321
North Dakota	North Dakota Board of Medical Examiners	418 East Rosser Avenue Bismarck, North Dakota 58501	701-233-9485
Ohio	Ohio State Medical Board	65 South Front Street, Suite 510 Columbus, Ohio 43215	614-466-3934
Oklahoma	Oklahoma State Board of Medical Examiners	P.O. Box 18256, Oklahoma City, Oklahoma 73154	405-848-6841
Oregon	Oregon Board of Medical Examiners	1002 Loyalty Building, 317 S.W. Alder Street Portland, Oregon 97204	503-229-5770
Pennsylvania	Pennsylvania Board of Medical Education and Licensure	P.O. Box 2649 Harrisburg, Pennsylvania 17105	717-787-2381
Rhode Island	Rhode Island Department of Health	104 Cannon Building, 75 Davis Street, Providence, Rhode Island 02908	401-277-2827
South Carolina	South Carolina State Board of Medical Examiners	1315 Blanding Street, Columbia, South Carolina 29201	803-758-3361
South Dakota	South Dakota State Board of Medical and Osteopathic Examiners	608 West Avenue North Sioux Falls, South Dakota 57104	605-336-1965
Tennessee	Tennessee State Board of Medical Examiners	320 R.S. Gass State Office Building, Ben Allen Road Nashville, Tennessee 37216	615-741-7280
Texas	Texas State Board of Medical Examiners	P.O. Box 13562 Capitol Station, Austin, Texas 78711	512-4475-0741
Utah	Utah Department of Registration	State Office Building, Room 5000 Salt Lake City, Utah 84114	801-268-6242

STATE	NAME	ADDRESS	TELEPHONE
Vermont	Vermont State Board of Medicine	109 State Street, Montpelier, Vermont 05602	802-828-2363
Virginia	Virginia State Board of Medicine	517 West Grace Street, Richmond, Virginia 23220	804-257-6497
Washington	Washington Department of Licensing	P.O. Box 9649, Olympia, Washington 98504	206-753-2205
West Virginia	West Virginia Board of Medicine	3412B Chesterfield Avenue, Charleston, West Virginia 25304	304-348-2971
Wisconsin	Wisconsin Medical Examining Board	1400 East Washington Avenue, Madison, Wisconsin 53702	608-266-2811
Wyoming	Wyoming Board of Medical Examiners	Hathaway Building, 4th Floor, Cheyenne, Wyoming 82002	307-777-7122

APPENDIX 3:
SAMPLE INFORMED CONSENT
AGREEMENT

I, [insert patient name] allow [insert physician name] to perform upon me an operation known as [type of operation to be performed, e.g., appendectomy, mastectomy, etc.]. I further understand that my physician may be assisted in performing this operation by [list names of any assisting physicians, if applicable], but that the operation will be primarily performed by [name of physician].

I have been informed that [insert physician name] has performed [#] [type of operation[s]] during the last 12 months and that the mortality rate was [xx%], the infection rate was [xx%] and the mistake rate was [xx%].

The hospital, [insert hospital name], has informed me that [#] related operations were performed during the last 12 months at this facility and that the mortality rate was [xx%], the infection rate was [xx%], and the mistake rate was [xx%].

My physician, [insert physician name], and this hospital, [insert hospital name], carry liability insurance in the amount of [insert dollar amount] and [insert dollar amount] respectively. This liability insurance [is/is not] approximately the same as other physicians and hospitals performing this operation would be expected to carry to provide compensation to patients who may die or be injured by medical mismanagement.

I have been informed that a [type of operation] is a (major/minor) operation and will be performed as described below:

[Describe in detail the procedure to be performed as well as the physician's rights to perform further surgery if an unexpected condition is encountered during the course of the surgery].

As with any major surgery, bleeding can occur and at times can be serious. In addition, infection can occur and the risks of developing such an infection are as reported above. [Describe all further risks of the procedure in detail].

I have been informed that the recovery period for this type of operation is as follows. [Describe details of recovery period].

I have been advised that a [type of operation] is necessary because [provide details as to why the particular procedure is necessary].

I have been advised that the alternatives of treatment include [provide details of all alternative treatments available, including the possible outcome and risks associated with the alternative treatments].

I have been advised that it is the opinion of my physician that a [type of operation] is indicated and the risks of the operation are less than the alternatives, and I have been given the opportunity of seeking independent consultation prior to having this surgery.

Although I have been fully informed about the risks of undergoing a [type of procedure], I am willing to undergo the operation. This does not relieve my physician of any responsibilities for acts of negligence, which would include rendering substandard care to me, causing injuries that should not have occurred, even though I am aware that there may be a risk in having the operation performed. I agree to undergo a [type of operation] after being fully informed, but expect that proper care shall be rendered to me at all times. This includes post-operative care by my physicians and the nurses and hospital personnel.

SIGNATURE LINE/DATE - PATIENT

SIGNATURE LINE/DATE - PHYSICIAN

APPENDIX 4:
RISKS ASSOCIATED WITH COMMON
MEDICAL PROCEDURES

PROCEDURE	POSSIBLE COMPLICATIONS
Adenoidectomy	Bleeding; Nasal speech; Nasal regurgitation of food or liquids
Anesthesia	Abnormal reaction to drugs; Aspiration of stomach contents; Injury to vocal cords or throat; Injury to teeth; lips; and tongue; Brain damage; Malignant hyperthermia
Angiography, cerebral	Injury to the arteries entered; Bleeding at the site of entry by catheter; Stroke; Blindness or brain damage; Emboli to the brain; Allergic reaction to the injected contrast medium
Angiography, coronary	Injury to the artery; Damage to heart; myocardial infarction; Possible need for open heart surgery; Irregular heartbeat; Bleeding at the site of entrance; Allergic reaction to injected contrast medium
Angioplasty	Paraplegia; Loss of extremity; Bowel infarction; Renal failure
Aortic Dissection	Stroke; Renal failure; Bowel infarction; Paraplegia; Death
Aortic Graft	Bleeding or Infection; Infection or emboli; Kidney failure or loss of limb; Inadequate blood to bowel or spinal cord; Myocardial infarction; Sexual dysfunction; Death
Appendectomy	Infection; Bleeding; Intra-abdominal abscess; Leakage from the colon requiring colostomy; Hernia in the incision

PROCEDURE	POSSIBLE COMPLICATIONS
Arteriovenous Shunt for Hemodialysis	Bleeding or infection; Damage blood vessel with risk of rupture; Recurrent thrombosis; Severe edema of extremity; Inadequate blood supply to extremity; Inadequate blood supply to nerves
Blood Transfusion	Fever; Kidney failure; Heart failure; Hepatitis; Aids
Breast Augmentation	Risks of use of silicon gel are excluded; Scar formation around implant causing hard breast; Deflation of implant; Loss of sensation to the nipple and breast; Persistent pain in breast; Distortion of breast mound; Leakage of implant contents
Breast Biopsy, excisional	Infection and/or blood clot; Failure to obtain accurate diagnosis; Disfiguring scar; Failure to locate and remove abnormality
Cardiopulmonary Bypass	Stroke; Respiratory complications; Kidney failure; Death
Carotid Endarterectomy	Blood clots; Infection; Stroke; Nerve injury causing mouth; throat; or tongue problems; Myocardial infarction; Death
Cataract Surgery	Loss of vision or decrease in vision; Loss of eye; Bleeding inside or behind eye; Painful eye; Droopy eyelid
Catheterization, central venous	Hemorrhage into chest cavity or elsewhere; Pericardial tamponade (compression of heart); Cardiac arrest or stroke; Collapse of lung; Damage to blood vessels; Infusion of fluid into chest cavity
Cervix Removal	Uncontrollable leakage of urine; Injury to the bladder; Injury to the bowel or intestinal obstruction; Injury to the ureter; Sterility; Pulmonary embolism
Childbirth	Injury to bladder; Injury to rectum; Fistula between vagina and rectum; Hemorrhage possibly requiring hysterectomy; Brain damage to fetus
Cholecystectomy	Pancreatitis; Injury to the bile duct; Retained stones in the bile duct; Narrowing of the bile duct; Injury to the bowel
Coarctation of Aorta	Quadriplegia or paraplegia; Permanent hoarseness; Leakage of body fluid from intestines into chest; Loss of bowel and/or bladder function; Impotence in males

PROCEDURE	POSSIBLE COMPLICATIONS
Colon Surgery	Infection of the incision; Intra-abdominal abscess; Leakage from colon and possible colostomy; Injury to other organs or blood vessels; Diarrhea—sometimes permanent; Formation of scar tissue causing intestinal blockage; Hernia in incision
Colonoscopy	Infection or bleeding; Perforation of colon or rectal wall; Cardiac arrhythmias
Dental Implants	Infection; bleeding; failure to heal; Permanent and disfiguring scarring; Premature loss of implant; or mobility; Loss of bone; Numbness of face or mouth; Fracture of jaw; Injury to adjacent teeth or sinus
Dilation and Curettage	Hemorrhage with possible hysterectomy; Perforation of the uterus; Injury to the bowel or bladder; Sterility
Ear Tubes	Persistent infection; Perforation of eardrum or cyst behind the eardrum; Need to surgically remove tubes
Endoscopic Retrograde Cholangio Pancreatogram (ERCP)	Infection; Perforation of esophagus; stomach; or intestines; Cardiac arrhythmias; Pancreatic inflammation
Endoscopy, abdominal	Puncture of the bowel or blood vessel; Abdominal infection; Operation to correct injury; Injury to ureter; Injury to bladder
Epidural, spinal	Abnormal reaction to drugs; Leakage of cerebrospinal fluid; Epidural blood clot or abscess; Broken needles or catheters; Incomplete analgesia; Back pain and/or paralysis; Severe headaches
Femoral Bypass Grafts	Bleeding requiring reoperation; Necrosis of skin around incision; Thrombi or emboli; Limb loss; Nerve damage; Myocardial infarction; Death
Fibroid Removal	Uncontrollable leakage of urine; Injury to bladder; Injury to the ureter; Injury to the bowel and/or intestinal obstruction; Sterility; Pulmonary embolism
Gastrectomy	Infection of incision or inside abdomen; Bleeding requiring transfusion; Leakage from stomach; Inability to maintain weight; Chronic vomiting after eating; Diarrhea and need for vitamin B-12 injections; Recurrence of condition for which surgery was done

PROCEDURE	POSSIBLE COMPLICATIONS
Hemodialysis	Hypotension; hemorrhage; sepsis; cardiac arrhythmias; Allergic reaction to tubing and dialyzer; Pulmonary edema; air bubbles in the bloodstream; seizure; hypothermia; fever; metabolic disorders; Viral infections such as HIV; Cardiac arrest
Hemorrhoidectomy	Bleeding; Post operative pain; especially with bowel movements; Temporary/permanent difficulty controlling bowels or gas; Recurrence of hemorrhoids; Narrowing of anal opening requiring repeated dialations
Hernia Repair	Infection; Bleeding; Recurrence of hernia; Injury to or loss of testicle or spermatic cords; Nerve injury resulting in numbness or chronic pain
Hysterectomy, abdominal or vaginal	Uncontrollable leakage of urine; Injury to bladder; Injury to ureter; Injury to the bowel and/or intestinal obstruction; Painful intercourse; Ovarian failure requiring hormone administration; Formation of fistula between vagina and rectum
Kidney Stone Lithotripsy	Bleeding in or around kidney; Obstruction of kidney by stone particles; Failure to completely fragment stones; High blood pressure; Loss of kidney
Liver Biopsy	Bleeding; Lung collapse; Internal leakage of bile; Puncture of other organs; Aspiration pheumonia
Lumpectomy	Infection or blood clot; Disfiguring scar; Fluid collection in arm pit; Numbness to arm; Swelling of arm; Damage to nerves of arm or chest; Recurrence of cancer
Mastectomy, radical	Limitation of movement of shoulder or arm; Swelling of the arm; Loss of skin requiring graft; Failure to eradicate the malignancy; Injury to major blood vessel
Oral Surgery	Infection; bleeding; failure to heal; Injury to adjacent teeth; Numbness of face and/or mouth; Fracture of either jaw; Opening between mouth and sinus or nose; Tooth fragment in sinus; Dry socket
Penile Implant	Bleeding and infection; Penile pain or numbness; Injury to bladder or urethra; Problems with implantable prosthetic
Prostatectomy	Bleeding and/or infection; Injury to bladder; urethra; or rectum; Impotence; Retrograde ejaculation; Bladder blockage; Incontinence

PROCEDURE	POSSIBLE COMPLICATIONS
Radial Keratotomy	Loss of vision or decrease in vision; Loss of eye; Variable vision; Radiating images around lights; Over or under correction; Cataract formation; Retained need for glasses
Radiation Therapy, head/neck- initial reaction	Altered sense of smell; taste; or nausea; Difficulty swallowing; weight loss; fatigue; Hoarseness; cough; loss of voice; Hearing loss; dizziness; Dry and irritable eyes; Increased risk of infection and/or bleeding; Intensified by chemotherapy
Radiation Therapy, head/neck-late reaction	Tooth decay and gum changes; Bone damage in jaws; Hair loss; scarring of skin; Swelling of tissues under chin; Brain; spinal cord or nerve damage; Pituitary or thyroid gland damage; Second cancers developing
Radiation Therapy, thorax-initial reaction	Skin changes; hair loss on the chest; Inflammation of the esophagus; heart sac; or lungs; Bleeding or fistula from tumor destruction; Intermittent electric shock-like feeling in the lower body; Increased risk of infection or bleeding; Intensified by chemotherapy
Radiation Therapy, thorax-late reaction	Changes in skin texture; scarring; hair loss; Lung scarring or shrinkage; Narrowing of esophagus; Constriction of heart sac; Damage to heart muscle or arteries; Fracture of ribs; Spinal cord or liver damage
Radical Mastectomy	Limitation of shoulder or arm movement; Swelling of the arm; Loss of the skin of the chest; Failure to completely eradicate the malignancy; Decreased sensation or numbness; Injury to major blood vessels
Renal Biopsy	Injury to adjacent organs; Infection; Hypotension; Bleeding from the kidney; Intestinal perforation.
Rhinoplasty	Bleeding; Infection; Disappointing cosmetic result; Impaired breathing through nose; Septal perforation
Septoplasty	Bleeding; Infection; Injury to nerve of upper teeth; Septal perforation; Spinal fluid leak
Sigmoidoscopy	Infection or bleeding; Perforation of colon or rectal wall; Cardiac arrhythmia

PROCEDURE	POSSIBLE COMPLICATIONS
Sinus Surgery	Bleeding; Infection; Scar formation; Spinal fluid leak; Infection of brain tissue; Blindness or eye damage; Injury to sense of smell
Spinal Manipulation	Stroke; Disc herniation; Soft tissue injury; Rib fracture
Spinal Operation	Pain; numbness or paralysis; Weakness in extremities; Loss of bladder function; Loss of bowel function; Unstable spine; Recurrence of condition; Injury to blood vessels
Thyroidectomy	Permanent hoarseness or impaired speech; Low blood calcium levels requiring extensive medication; Life long requirement of thyroid medication
Tonsillectomy	Bleeding; Injury to nerves to tongue; Nasal speech
Vasectomy	Bleeding and/or infection; Testicular swelling or pain; Spermatic Granuloma (nodule in cord at site of surgery); Reconnection of vas tube resulting in fertility
Ventriculoperitoneal Shunt	Heart failure; Infection in blood stream; Occlusion of large veins in chest; Blood or fluid collection around heart; Blood clots in the lung
Ventriculoperitoneal Shunt Placement	Malfunction of shunt due to infection; Collection of blood or fluid between brain and skull; Headaches; Development of need for another shunt; Blood clot in brain; Blindness; seizures or epilepsy; Leaks or separation of catheter

NOTE: The risks listed above are taken from the rules of the Louisiana Department of Health and Hospitals. The risks were defined by the Louisiana Medical Disclosure Panel and are required to be disclosed by physicians to patients. The Louisiana Medical Disclosure Panel Law requires that physicians tell patients (1) the nature of the patient's condition (2) the general nature of the proposed treatment/surgery (3) the risks of the proposed treatment/surgery; as defined by the Panel; and (4) reasonable therapeutic alternatives and risks associated with such alternatives. ARM suggests patients discuss these risks with your doctors and ask how often the risks have occurred in his/her practice before undergoing any procedure.

Source: The Association for Responsible Medicine

APPENDIX 5:
DONOR'S STATEMENT REGARDING
ANATOMICAL GIFTS

I, [insert donor's name and address], make the following statement regarding anatomical gifts.

ANATOMICAL GIFT

I give such parts of my body to such individuals, institutions, or physicians, qualified to receive anatomical gifts under [specify applicable section of the Uniform Anatomical Gifts Act or the state law governing anatomical gifts], as may be requested by such individuals, institutions, or physicians. I request that my personal representative or an authorized person make anatomical gifts in a manner consistent with my desires expressed in this statement, and I request that my next of kin respect my wishes.

PRIORITY OF DONATIONS

An anatomical gift that will be used in connection with the treatment of an imminently life threatening disorder shall take precedence over a gift of that part to any other donee. My personal representative or an authorized person shall make final determination of who is to receive any part if a conflict should arise.

ATTENDING PHYSICIAN

If my attending physician accepts an anatomical gift on behalf of a donee, that physician shall not participate in the procedure for removing or transplanting such part.

INSTRUCTIONS

If I have given any written instructions regarding the burial, cremation, or other disposition of my body, I direct that any donee take possession of my body subject to such instructions, if that donee has actual knowledge of such instructions. If there is any conflict between the statements made in this document and such instructions, my wishes regarding anatomical gifts shall take preference over my instructions regarding the disposition of my body.

COUNTERPARTS

I may be signing more than one statement regarding anatomical gifts. I intend that only signed documents be effective and that no effect shall be given to a photocopy or other reproduction of a signed document.

DEFINITIONS

The term "part," "physician," and "attending physician" have the same meaning as is given to these terms in the [specify applicable section of the Uniform Anatomical Gifts Act or the state law governing anatomical gifts]. The term "authorized person" means a person authorized to make donations under [specify applicable section of the Uniform Anatomical Gifts Act or the state law governing anatomical gifts], in the order of priority provided in that statute.

EXPENSES

I make this gift on the condition that the gift be made at no expense to my estate or my family. All expenses or costs associated with the gift shall be borne by the donee or recipient or an individual or entity on the donee's or recipient's behalf.

Signed in the presence of the witnesses who have signed below this _____ day of _____, 20__.

SIGNATURE LINE – DONOR

SIGNATURE LINE - WITNESS #1

SIGNATURE LINE - WITNESS #2

NOTARIAL ACKNOWLEDGMENT

BEFORE ME, the undersigned authority, on this day personally appeared [insert name of donor], and [names of two witnesses], known to me to be the declarant and witnesses whose names are subscribed to the foregoing instrument in their respective capacities, and, all of said persons being by me duly sworn, [name of donor] declared to me and to the said witnesses in my presence that said instrument is (his/her) Statement Regarding Anatomical Gifts, and that (he/she) had willingly and voluntarily made and executed it as (his/her) free act and deed for the purposes therein expressed.

SUBSCRIBED AND SWORN TO BEFORE ME by the declarant, [insert name] and by the witnesses [insert names] this ＿＿ day of ＿＿＿＿＿ ＿＿＿＿＿＿＿, 20＿＿.

SIGNATURE LINE - NOTARY PUBLIC

APPENDIX 6:
STATE STATUTES GOVERNING JOINT AND SEVERAL LIABILITY IN MEDICAL MALPRACTICE CASES

JURISDICTION	STATUTE	APPLICABLE PROVISION
Alabama	None	None
Alaska	Alaska Statutes, § 09.17.080(d)	Multiple defendants liable only for their percentage of fault.
Arizona	Arizona Revised Statutes, § 12-2506	Multiple defendants liable only for their proportion of fault unless acting in concert or in an agency relationship.
Arkansas	None	None
California	California Civil Procedure Code, § 1431.2	The liability of multiple defendants for noneconomic damages shall be in direct proportion to each defendant's proportion of fault.
Colorado	Colorado Revised Statutes, § 13-21-111.5	Procedures in section 13-20-602 which require plaintiff to file a certificate of review within 60 days after service of complaint shall apply if negligence or fault of nonparty is considered and nonparty is a licensed health care professional.

JURISDICTION	STATUTE	APPLICABLE PROVISION
Connecticut	Connecticut General Statutes Annotated, § 52-572a	Multiple defendants liable only for their proportionate share of fault unless award from any one defendant is uncollectible. In the event that recovery from one or more defendants is unrecoverable, the court will assess remaining defendants for a proportionate share of the uncollectible amount for noneconomic and economic damages.
Delaware	None	None
District of Columbia	None	None
Florida	Florida Statutes Annotated, § 768.81	Where damage award exceeds $25,000, the court will order multiple defendants to pay according to their respective proportion of fault, provided that with respect to any party whose fault equals or exceeds that of a particular plaintiff, court shall enter judgment on basis of doctrine of joint and several liability.
Georgia	Georgia Code, § 51-12-32, 33	Where the plaintiff is to some degree responsible for the injury, the jury may apportion the award of damages among the persons liable for the injury whose fault is greater than the plaintiff's. Where the jury so apportions liability for purposes of calculating damage payments, other defendants in the suit may not treat the liability as a joint one. Except where prohibited, contribution may be enforced among joint tortfeasors.
Hawaii	None	None
Idaho	Idaho Code, § 6-803	Where multiple defendants act in concert, or one defendant is the agent of another, there is a right of contribution between joint tortfeasors.
Illinois	735 ILCS 5/2-1117, 1118	Defendants are joint and severally liable only if defendant's negligence exceeds 25% of total fault attributable to plaintiff.
Indiana	None	None

JURISDICTION	STATUTE	APPLICABLE PROVISION
Iowa	Code of Iowa, § 668.4	Defendants whose liability is less than 50% of the total fault assigned to all parties are liable only for their proportion of fault.
Kansas	None	None
Kentucky	Kentucky Revised Statutes, § 411.182	Defendants are liable only for their proportion of fault.
Louisiana	None	None
Maine	None	None
Maryland	None	None
Massachusetts	None	None
Michigan	Michigan Comp. Laws, § 600.6304	Defendants shall be required to pay damages equal to their respective portions of fault. If part or all of defendant's liability is uncollectible, this portion of the judgment will be reallocated among remaining defendants according to their respective portions of fault in the case.
Minnesota	Minnesota Statutes, § 604.02	A person whose fault ins 15% or less may be jointly liable for a percentage of the whole award no greater than four times his percentage of fault.
Mississippi	Mississippi Code Annotated, § 85-5-7	Multiple defendants shall be liable in proportion to their fault, except that liability of multiple defendants shall be joint to the extent necessary for the plaintiff to recover 50% of his damages. Multiple defendants will also be jointly liable if they act in concert. In assessing percentages of fault, an employer and employee shall be considered as one defendant where employer's liability rests upon employee's negligence.
Missouri	Missouri Revised Statutes, § 538.230	Multiple defendants shall be jointly liable only with those defendants whose apportioned percentage of fault is equal to or less than such defendant.

JURISDICTION	STATUTE	APPLICABLE PROVISION
Montana	Montana Code Annotated, § 27-1-703	Any party whose fault is 50% or less of the combined negligence of all parties is liable only for his hare of the fault. The remaining parties are jointly and severally liable. Parties are jointly liable if they act in concert or as an agent of another.
Nebraska	Revised Statutes of Nebraska, § 44-21,185,10	Economic and non-economic damages shall be joint and several in cases involving two or more defendants acting in concert. In other actions involving more than one defendant
Nevada	Nevada Revised Statutes, § 41.141	Where there are multiple defendants in a negligence action, each defendant is severally liable only for those damages equal to the proportion of fault attributable to each defendant, unless defendants have acted in concert. Concerted acts of the defendant does not include negligent acts committed by providers of health care while working together to provide treatment.
New Hampshire	New Hampshire Revised Statutes Annotated, § 507:7e	If any party shall be less than 50% at fault, then that party's liability shall be several and shall be proportionate to their individual fault, except where parties acting in concert.
New Jersey	New Jersey Revised Statutes, § 2A:15-5.3	Parties who are 60% or more responsible for total damages are jointly and severally liable; parties who are at least 20% but less than 60% responsible are liable jointly and severally for the full amount of economic damages plus their proportion of fault for non-economic damages; parties liable for 20% or less of total damages are liable only for their proportion of fault.
New Mexico	New Mexico Statutes Annotated, § 41-3A-1	In any cause of action where comparative negligence applies, liability of joint tortfeasors shall be several and determined according to each defendant's proportion of fault. Joint and several liability applies only to a defendant acting intentionally, to defendants in an agency relationship, in a product liability action, or where public policy is served by application of the rule.

JURISDICTION	STATUTE	APPLICABLE PROVISION
New York	N.Y. Consolidated Laws, Art. 16 § 1601(1)	Where joint tortfeasor found to be 50% or less liable, non-economic loss shall not exceed defendant's equitable share.
North Carolina	None	None
North Dakota	North Dakota Cent. Code, § 32-03.2-02	Only multiple defendants found to have acted in concert or encouraged or adopted tortious act for their benefit are jointly liable for all damages attributable to their combined percentage of fault. All others severally liable.
Ohio	Ohio Revised Code Annotated, § 2315.19	Each party jointly and severally liable for economic damages. for noneconomic damages, where plaintiff contributorily negligent, each defendant is liable only for his proportionate share of fault.
Oklahoma	None	None Oregon
Pennsylvania	None	None
Rhode Island	Rhode Island General Laws, § 10-6-2	Two or more persons jointly or severally liable in tort for the same injury. Applicable to physicians.
South Carolina	South Carolina Code Annotated, § 15-38-10	Joint tortfeasors severally liable only according to their proportionate fault.
South Dakota	South Dakota Codified Laws Annotated, § 15-8- 15.1	Any defendant allocated less than 50% of the total fault allocated to all the parties may not be jointly liable for more than twice the percentage of fault allocated to that party.
Tennessee	None	None
Texas	Texas Civil Practice Code Annotated, § 33.013	Defendants are jointly and severally liable only where the percentage of responsibility is greater than 20% and is greater than the plaintiff's responsibility, or where the defendant's responsibility is greater than 10% and the plaintiff has no responsibility.
Utah	Utah Code Annotated, § 78-27-40	Defendant severally liable only in proportion to amount of fault attributed to that defendant.

JURISDICTION	STATUTE	APPLICABLE PROVISION
Vermont	None	None
Virginia	None	None
Washington	Washington Revised Code Annotated, § 4.22.070	Liability of each defendant shall be joint only if parties acted in concert or their was an agency relationship, or if the jury determines that the plaintiff was not at fault, the defendants shall be jointly and severally liable for the sum of their proportionate shares of plaintiff's total damages.
West Virginia	West Virginia Code, §55-7B-9	Defendants in medical injury suits bearing more than 25% of the liability shall be jointly and severally liable. Wisconsin
Wyoming	Wyoming Statutes, § 1-1-109	Each default.

Source: Compendium of Selected State Laws Governing Medical Injury Claims, U.S. Department of Health and Human Services.

APPENDIX 7:
STATE STATUTES GOVERNING LIMITS ON DAMAGE AWARDS IN MEDICAL MALPRACTICE CASES

JURISDICTION	STATUTE	APPLICABLE PROVISION
Alabama	Alabama Code, § 6-5-544; 547	$400,000 limit on non-economic damages including punitive damages; $1 million limit on wrongful death actions.
Alaska	Alaska Statutes, § 09.17.010	Noneconomic losses may not exceed $500,000 but this limit does not apply to damages for disfigurement or severe physical impairment.
Arizona	Arizona State Constitution, Article 2, § 31	No law shall be enacted limiting damages for death or injury.
Arkansas	None	None California
Colorado	Colorado Revised Statutes, § 13-64-302.5; 13-21- 203; 13-64-302	Plaintiff may not recover exemplary damages against a physician for adverse outcome of prescription drug or product where regulatory protocol followed; permissible recovery for wrongful death limited to $250,000; total recovery shall not exceed $1 million dollars, noneconomic los shall not exceed $1250,000. Court has discretion to increase recovery in certain situations.
Connecticut	None	None

JURISDICTION	STATUTE	APPLICABLE PROVISION
Delaware	Delaware Code Annotated, Title 18, § 6855	Punitive damages may be awarded upon finding of malicious intent to injure or wilful or wanton misconduct.
District of Columbia	None	None
Florida	Florida Statutes Annotated, § 768.80	Damages for noneconomic losses may not exceed $450,000.
Georgia	None	None
Hawaii	None	None
Idaho	Idaho Code, § 6-1603	Noneconomic damages shall not exceed $400,000 unless personal injury caused by willful or reckless misconduct or circumstances that would constitute a felony. This cap shall increase or decrease yearly according to the state's adjustment of the average annual wage.
Illinois	None	None
Indiana	None	None
Iowa	None	None
Kansas	Kansas Statutes Annotated, §60-19a02	In any personal injury action, the total amount recoverable by each party from all defendants for all claims for noneconomic loss shall not exceed $250,000. Applies to claims accruing on or after July 1.
Kentucky	None	None
Louisiana	Louisiana Revised Statutes Annotated, §40:1299.42	The total amount of damages for all malpractice claims may not exceed $500,000 plus interest and costs exclusive of future medical care and related benefits; health care provider liable for up to $100,000 and state Patient Compensation Fund liable for remainder.
Maine	None	None
Maryland	Maryland Courts & Judicial Procedure Code Annotated, § 11.108	In any action for damages for personal injury accruing after July 1.

JURISDICTION	STATUTE	APPLICABLE PROVISION
Massachusetts	Massachusetts General laws Annotated, Chapter 231, § 60H	The plaintiff shall be awarded no more than $500,000 for non-economic damages unless the jury determines that there is a substantial or permanent loss or impairment of bodily function or substantial disfigurement, or other special circumstances which warrant a finding that the cap was unfair. If the total amount of general damages from a single occurrence for all plaintiffs exceeds $500,000, then the amount of such damages recoverable by each plaintiff will be reduced to a percentage of $500,000 proportionate to that plaintiff's share of the total amount of such damages for all plaintiffs.
Michigan	Michigan Comp. Laws, § 600.1483	Damages for noneconomic loss shall not exceed $225,000 unless there has been a death, intentional tort, foreign object wrongfully left in body, injury to reproductive system, fraudulent concealment of injury by health care provider, limb or organ wrongfully removed and patient has lost a vital bodily function. The limit on noneconomic damages shall be increased each year by the increase in the consumer price index.
Minnesota	Minnesota Statutes, § 549,20	Punitive damages may be awarded only upon a showing of willful indifference or deliberate disregard for care.
Mississippi	None	None
Missouri	Missouri Revised Statutes, § 538.210	No plaintiff in an action against health care provider shall recover more than $350,000 per occurrence for noneconomic damages from any one defendant. This limit shall be increased or decreased on an annual basis effective January 1st of each year in accordance with figures determined by the U.S. Department of Commerce.

JURISDICTION	STATUTE	APPLICABLE PROVISION
Montana	Montana Code Annotated, § 27-1-7310	Recovery of non-economic damages prohibited in breach of contract action unless breach caused physical injury.
Nebraska	Revised Statutes of Nebraska, § 44-2825	The total amount recoverable by a plaintiff against a health care provider, including amounts from the Excess Liability Fund, may not exceed $1,250,000. The health care provider liability limited to $200,000 and state Patient Compensation Fund pays the balance.
Nevada	None	None
New Hampshire	New Hampshire Revised Statutes Annotated, § 508:4-d	Damages for noneconomic loss shall not exceed $875,000.
New Jersey	None	None
New Mexico	New Mexico Statutes Annotated, § 41-5-6	Limit for aggregate dollar amount recoverable is $600,000; health care provider liability limit is $200,000 and balance from state Patient Compensation Fund.
New York	None	None
North Carolina	None	None
North Dakota	North Dakota Cent. Code, § 32-03.2-08	Any party responsible for payment of any part of an award for economic damages may request a review by the Court of the reasonableness of any award in excess of $250,000.
Ohio	None	None
Oklahoma	None	None
Oregon	Oregon Revised Statutes, § 18.560; 550	The amount awarded for noneconomic damages in a personal injury action may not exceed $500,000; no punitive damages awarded against licensed physician who is acting within scope of license without malice.
Pennsylvania	None	None
Rhode Island	None	None

JURISDICTION	STATUTE	APPLICABLE PROVISION
South Carolina	South Carolina Code Annotated, § 15-78-120	Liability of health care provider employed by government is limited to $1 million dollars unless services giving rise to claims were rendered with expectation or receipt of payment beyond salary.
South Dakota	South Dakota Codified Laws Annotated, § 21-3- 11	Total damages awarded by court or through binding arbitration may not exceed $1 million dollars.
Tennessee	None	None
Texas	None	None
Utah	Utah Code Annotated, § 78-14-7.1	Noneconomic losses may not exceed $250,000.
Vermont	None	None
Virginia	Virginia Code, § 8.01-581.15	Damages recoverable by plaintiff in medical injury suit are limited to $1 million dollars.
Washington	None	None
West Virginia	West Virginia Code, §55-7B-8	Noneconomic damages shall not exceed $1 million dollars and the jury must be so instructed.
Wisconsin	Wisconsin Statutes, § 893.55	Noneconomic damages may not exceed $1 million dollars. This limit shall be annually adjusted to reflect changes in the consumer price index.
Wyoming	None	None

Source: Compendium of Selected State Laws Governing Medical Injury Claims, U.S. Department of Health and Human Services.

APPENDIX 8:
COMMONLY USED MEDICAL TERMINOLOGY

COMMON MEDICAL TERMS

Active Motion: A voluntary movement made by a person, or the extent to which he will move a member of his body.

Adhesion: The uniting of one surface with another by scar tissue.

Aneurysm: A dilation, or saccule formation, of an artery. The source may be congenital, luetic, or arteriosclerotic.

Angina: Refers to pain in the heart, usually associated with physical effort. It is due, in most instances, to inadequate blood supply to the heart muscle.

Angiography: The visualization of blood vessels by the use of X-ray and the injection of some form of contrast material.

Ankylosis: Complete or partial loss of motion in a joint; the union of bones forming a joint causing a stiff joint.

Anterior - Posterior: Front to back.

Apposition: The fitting together.

Aphakia: Absence of the lens of the eye.

Aphasia: Loss of power of speech; inability to talk.

Arteriosclerosis or atherosclerosis: So-called "hardening of the arteries." A degenerative condition in which the walls of the arteries lose their elasticity and at times become calcified. As a result, there may be some restriction of blood flow.

Arthrodesis: An operative procedure to eliminate a joint and cause fusion of two adjacent bones.

Arthrography: The visualization of the interior of a joint by use of contrast material and X-ray.

Arthroplasty: An operative procedure to restore motion to a joint

Arthroscope: A surgical instrument that can be inserted into a joint through a small incision, allowing visualization of the interior of the joint, and allowing surgical procedures of certain types.

Cartilaginous Discs: Plates which act as shock absorbers between the bones of the vertebrae along the spine.

Cerebral Concussion: A minute and diffuse injury to the brain caused by direct or indirect violence. A diagnostic symptom is a loss of consciousness of momentary to prolonged degree. There is often a transient, or permanent, loss of memory for detail preceding the accident for a short time. Symptoms of dizziness or headache, known as the "post-concussion syndrome," may persist for some time, without any objective neurological evidence of damage.

Cervical Spine: The seven upper vertebrae of the spine located in the neck.

Closed Reduction: A reduction accomplished by manipulation or traction without opening the site of the fracture.

Coccyx: The tailbone located in the distal end of the sacrum.

Comminuted Fracture: A fracture in which there are multiple breaks within a given bone resulting in more than two bone pieces or fragments.

Complete Dislocation: A dislocation in which normal contact of one bone with another is entirely lost and one bone is completely separated from any joint contact with the other bone.

Compound Fracture: A fracture in which there is a wound caused either by bone end puncturing the skin or by external force.

Compression Fracture: A fracture in which the bones are violently forced together.

Contact Dermatitis: A skin condition secondary to exposure to some substance for which the patient possesses an allergy or sensitivity.

Coronary Heart Disease: A disease process of the arteries that supply the heart causing chest pain or heart muscle damage, which derives from degenerative changes in the tissue of the artery wall. It is believed to bear a relationship to arteriosclerosis.

CT Scan: "CT stands for "Computerized Tomography." A special X-ray technique which, combined with the computer, allows visualization of the internal parts of the body in better detail than in ordinary X-ray study. At times it is used with injection of contrast materials.

Cystoscope: An instrument to examine the interior of the urinary bladder.

Delayed Union: A union in which the soft union does not harden in the average time but finally solidifies.

Depression Fracture: A fracture in which the bone is driven inward, usually in the skull or face.

Dislocation: Displacement of an organ or joint surfaces.

Distal: Farthest away from the body.

Empyema: A collection of pus within the pleural cavity.

Exploratory: In reference to surgery, means that the diagnosis prior to operation is not too definite, and that actual visualization of pathology is necessary to effect a correct diagnosis.

Fibrous Union - A union in which nature heals the fracture partially but the line and bone cells do not harden resulting in an unsatisfactory healing where the member is not of much use and will not support weight.

Foot-drop: An inability to dorsiflex or raise the foot, which results in a dragging gait, and is indicative of pathology involving the peroneal nerve.

Fracture: An interruption in the normal continuity of a bone.

Functional: In reference to disease, infers that no organic pathology can be found.

Good Firm Body Union: A union in which there is normal healing of a fracture.

Green Stick Fracture: A crack or break not extending completely through the bone.

Herniated Disc: A disc which bulges beyond the edges of the vertebrae and presses against spinal nerves.

Hyperesthesia: Descriptive of an increase in skin sensation.

Hypesthesia (Hypoesthesia): Descriptive of a decrease in skin sensation.

Impacted Fracture: A fracture in which the bones are driven together and held solidly.

Incomplete Dislocation: A dislocation in which the displacement of the bone has only partially occurred with still a portion of one bone end in contact with the other.

Intervertebral Disc: A plate lying between each of the vertebrae consisting of a central core of firm, jelly-like material which acts as a cushion between the vertebrae.

IVP: An abbreviation for "intravenous pyelogram," in which a dye is injected into a vein and the kidney outline is apparent on an X-ray.

Joint-mice: Presence of cartilaginous loose bodies free within a joint cavity.

Laceration: A tear or wound in the soft tissue or skin.

Laminectomy: A surgical procedure removing part, or all, or the lamina of the vertebrae. The lamina is the bony strut that stands between the body and the spinous process on each side and encloses the spinal canal. The term is sometimes used to indicate the operation for removal of a ruptured, or herniated, intervertebral disc.

Lateral: From the side.

Loose Bodies: This term is used interchangeably with joint-mice.

Lumbar Spine: Five lumbar vertebrae located in the lower back.

Lymphadenitis: Inflammation of the lymph glands, secondary to infection.

Mal-Union: A union in which the bone fragments heal in a poor functional position or considerably at variance with the normal bone contour.

Meniscus: A small, crescent-shaped piece of cartilage found at the medial and lateral sides of the knee joint.

Myositis: Inflammation of a muscle.

Neuritis: Inflammation of a nerve.

Neurosis: A condition in which mental, or physical, symptoms may occur secondary to some form of subconscious conflict. Although in most cases no organic pathology can be found, the condition may progress to the point where physiological changes occur. A not uncommon condition, it is one that should be distinguished from malingering, that is, situations in which the individual consciously manufactures symptoms for monetary or other gain. A "traumatic neurosis" is the development of neurotic symptoms that have been precipitated by an accident or injury.

Non-Union: A union in which no bone structure reforms to span the area between the two bone fragments of the fracture resulting in a condition where only scar tissue holds the bone ends together.

Oblique: At an angle, midway between anterior-posterior and lateral.

Open Reduction: A reduction accomplished through a cutting operation to get the bones back in place which may include wiring, insertion of metal plates, one grafting, or tying the bones together.

Ophthalmology: The field of scientific information concerning the eye.

Organic: In reference to disease, organic means that there is actual tissue pathology as a source for the condition.

Otology: The field of scientific information regarding the ear.

Paracentesis: To remove fluid from within a cavity by means of a large needle.

Paralysis: This may be spastic or flaccid. In the flaccid type there is no voluntary control of the muscles involved, and they are in a completely relaxed condition with absence of muscle tone. In the spastic type there is usually no voluntary control, but the muscles remain in a chronic state of contraction and rigidity.

Paresis: This may refer to softening of the brain, such as may occur with syphilis, with a disturbance of mental function. The term is also frequently used to indicate a muscular weakness of neurologic origin, rather than complete paralysis.

Paresthesia: Abnormal skin sensation in the form of itching, prickling, burning, crawling sensations, etc.

Partial Union: A union in which the new bone does not adequately form to bridge the fracture site.

Passive Motion: Submissive motion or the extent to which the person will allow the member of his body to be moved by the examiner.

Pathological Fracture: A fracture caused by bone weakness.

Phlebitis: Inflammation of a vein.

Pleurisy: Inflammation of the covering membrane of the lungs.

Proximal: Closest to the body.

Psychosis: A severe form of mental illness in which the individual loses contact with reality.

Reduction: The setting of broken bones, or replacing of a dislocated joint, back to the normal condition.

Revision: In reference to surgery, to reconstruct or remodel.

Sacrum: The portion of the spine which joins the whole spine to the pelvis.

Shock: The state of physical collapse.

Simple Fracture: A fracture in which there is a single break in the continuity of the bone.

Spinal Tap: To remove spinal fluid by means of a needle.

Sprain: The result when muscles or ligaments are partially torn, joint fluids may escape, and nerves or blood vessels may be damaged.

Sprain Fracture: A fracture in which the bone is torn off by a tendon or ligament.

Strain: The excessive stretching or overuse of muscles or ligaments.

Tenosynovitis: Inflammation of a tendon and its sheath.

Thoracic Spine: Twelve thoracic vertebrae located in the upper back.

Traction: An arrangement of weights and pulleys to counteract the unsettling pull of muscles attached to a bone.

Transverse Laceration: A tear in which the tissue or skin is torn in a crosswise fashion.

Ultrasound: High-frequency sound waves which may be used for treatment, or diagnosis, of certain types of pathology.

Union: The process of healing of fractured bones.

Varicosity: Refers to varicose veins, meaning abnormal dilatation of certain portions of a vein. This usually leads to failure of valves within the vein and, secondarily, to interference with normal circulation.

Visual Field: An outline of the area of general vision when the eye is kept on a fixed point.

Whiplash: A sprain in the cervico-dorsal area.

COMMON PREFIXES USED IN MEDICAL TERMS

A or An–absence of

A or Ah–from, away

Ad–to, toward, near

Ambi–both

Ante–before

Anti–against

Auto–self

Bi–two

Circum–around

Contra–against, opposed

Counter–against

Di–two

Dis–the opposite of

Dys–difficult, painful

Ecto–outside

En–in

Eu–well

Ex or E–from, without

Exo–outside

Extra–outside

Glosso–relating to the tongue

Hemi–half

Hetero–other

Homo–same

Hydro–relating to water

Hyp–under or reduced

Hyper–above or excessive

Hypo–below or deficient

In–in

In–not

Infra–below

Inter–between

Intra–within

Lipo–relating to fat

Macro–large

Micro–small

Mon–single

Mult–much or many

Odont–teeth

Onych–nails

Osteo–pertaining to bone

Pare–faulty, related to

Per–throughout

Peri–around

Phleb–veins

Poly–many

Post–after

Pre–before

Pro–before

Pseud–false

Pulmo–relating to the lungs

Retro–backward

Scolio–twisted, bent

Semi–half

Sub–under

Super–above

Supra–above, upon

Sym or Syn–with, together

Trans–across

Tri–three

Uni–one

COMMON ROOTS USED IN MEDICAL TERMS

Aden–gland

Bio–life

Cardi–heart

Cephal–head

Chole–bile

Chondr–cartilage

Cost–rib

Crani–skull

Cyst–sac

Cyt–cell

Derm–skin

Encephal–brain

Enter–intestine

Gastr–stomach

Gynec–woman

Hem or hemat–blood

Hyster–uterus

Kerat–cornea

Leuc–white

My–muscle

Neph–kidney

Oopher–ovary

Ophthalm–eye

Oss or oste–bone

Ot–ear

Ovar–ovary

Path–disease

Ped–children

Ped–feet

Pneum–lung

Proct–anus

Psych–mind

Py–pus

Pyel–pelvis

Rhin–nose

Salping–tube

Septic–poison

Tox–poison

Trache–trachea

COMMON SUFFIXES USED IN MEDICAL TERMS

Algia–pain

Asis–condition, state

Asthenia–weakness

Cele–tumor, hemia

Cyte–cell

Ectasis–dilation

Ectomy–excision

Emia–blood

Esthesia–feeling, sensation

Genic–causing

Itis–inflammation

Logy–science of

Oma–tumor

Osis–condition, state

Ostomy–forming an opening

Otomy–cutting into

Patho–disease

Pathy–disease

Penia–insufficiency

Pexy–fixation

Phagia–eating

Phasia–speech

Phobia–fear

Plasty–molding

Pnea–breathing

Ptosis–falling

Rhythmia–rhythm

Rrhaphy–suture of

Uria–urine

HOSPITAL RECORD ABBREVIATIONS

AB–abortion

Abd–abdomen

AMA–against medical advice

a.c.–before meals

AMB–ambulate

Ad Lib–freely; as much as desired

adm.–admit

a.m.–before noon

AD–right ear

ADL–activities of daily living

A&P–anterior and posterior

b.i.d.–twice a day

B.M.–bowel movement

BMR–basal metabolic rate

BP–blood pressure

B.R.P.–bathroom privileges

BUE–both upper extremities

Bx–biopsy

CO2–carbon dioxide

C.OL.D.–chronic obstructive lung disease

C.O.P.D.–chronic obstructive pulmonary disease

CPPB–continuous positive pressure breathing; respirator

CSF–cerebral spinal fluid

CV–cardiovascular

CVA–cerebrovascular accident; stroke

CXR–chest x-ray

DB–diabetic

D&C–dilation & curettage

d/c–discontinue

disc.–discontinue

disch.–discharge

DKA–diabetic ketoacidosis

D/NS–dextrose 5% in normal saline

DOA–dead on arrival

DOE–dyspnea on exertion

D/S–dextrose in saline

D/W–dextrose in water

dx.–diagnose

D/5W–dextrose 5% in water

EBL–estimated blood loss

ECG–electrocardiogram

ECT–electroconvulsive therapy

EDC–estimated date of confinement

ED–emergency department

EEG–electroencephalogram

EENT–ears, eyes, nose and throat

EKG–electrocardiogram

EMG–electromyography

ENT–ear, nose and throat

EOM–extraocular movement

ER–emergency room

EST–electroshock therapy

ETH–elixir terpin hydrate

ETOH–alcohol

F/U–follow up

Fam. Hx–family history

FIB–fibrillation

fl. dr.–fluid dram

f.s.–frozen section

FUO–fever of undetermined origin

fx–fracture

GBS–gallbladder series

G.I.–gastrointestinal

GLUC–glucose

gr.–grain

GSW–gun shot wound

gtt–drop

G.U.–genito-urinary

H.–hour

h/a–headache

Hct.–hematocrit

H.E.E.N.T.–head, eyes, ears, nose, throat

Hg–mercury

Hgb.–hemoglobin

HH–hiatal hernia

H.N.P.–herniation of nucleus pulposus

h/o–history of

H2O–water

H&P–history and physical

HP–hot pack

HPI–history of present illness

/HR.–per hour

HR–hour

H.S.–hour of sleep

Hx–history

I–one

ii–two

ICF–intensive care facility

ICP–intracranial pressure

ICU–intensive care unnit

I&D–incision and drainage

IM–intramuscular

IMI–inferior myocardial infarct

I&O–intake and output

I.P.P.B.–intermittent positive pressure breathing; respirator

iss–one and one half

IV–intravenous

JVD–jugular vein distension

K–potassium

kg–kilogram

KUB–kidney, ureter, bladder

L–left

l–liter

LBBB–left bundle branch block

LBP–low back pain

LLE–left lower extremity

LLL–left lower lobe

LLQ–left lower quadrant

L.O.C.–loss of consciousness

LUE–left upper extremity

LUL–left upper lobe

LUQ–left upper quadrant

m–minim

Mg.–milligram

Mg/DL–milligrams per decileter

MI–myocardial infarction

min–minim

ml–milliliter

mm–millimeter

mmHg–millimeters of mercury

Na–sodium

NA–not applicable

n/a–not applicable

NaCl–sodium chloride; salt

NAD–no acute distress

N/G–nasogastric

NOS–no organism seen

NPO–nothing by mouth

NSR–normal sinus rhythm

n/v–nausea and vomiting

O2–oxygen

OM–otitis media

O.R.I.F.–open reduction and internal fixation

O.S.–left eye

O.T.–occupational therapy

O.U.–each eye

p–after

P–pulse

P&A–percussion and auscultation

p.c.–after meal

PCN–penicillin

P.E.–physical examination

PERLA–pupils equal and reactive to light and accommodation

PID–pelvic inflammatory disease

p.o.–by mouth

Pos–positive

PR–pulse rate

prn–as needed

pt–patient

PT–physical therapy

q–every

q.a.m.–every morning

q.d.–daily

q.h.–every hour

q.i.d.–four times a day

q.n.–every night

q.o.d.–every other day

q.p.m.–every night

RA–rheumatoid arthritis

RBBB–right bundle branch block

RBC–red blood count

RLE–right lower extremity

Rll–right lower lobe

RLQ–right lower quadrant

RML–right middle lobe

R/O–rule out

R.O.M.–range of motion

ROM–right otitis media

RR–recovery room

RUE–right upper extremity

RUQ–right upper quadrant

Rx–prescription

sc–subcutaneous

SIDS–sudden infant death syndrome

SLR–straight leg raises

SMAC–sequential multiple analyzer with computer

SOAP–subjective, objective, assessment, plan

SOB–shortness of breath

Soc. Hx.–social history

ss–one half

sub q–subcutaneous

Sx–signs, symptoms

SZ–seizure

t–teaspoon

T–tablespoon

T&A–tonsillectomy & adenoidectomy

T.A.H.–total abdominal hysterectomy

TENS–transcutaneous electrical nerve stimulation

Trach–tracheostomy

TUR–transurethral resection

TURP–transurethral resection of prostate

Tx–transfusion, transfer

U–unit

U/S–ultrasound

UE–upper extremity

UGIS–upper gastrointestinal series

URI–upper respiratory infection

U.T.I.–urinary tract infection

v–vomiting

VF–ventricular fibrillation

V.S.–vital signs

wbc–white blood cells

WBC–white blood count

wc–wheelchair

WD–well developed

WN–well nourished

WHP–whirlpool

WNL–within normal limits

x-match–cross match

X-S–excess

y/o–years old

APPENDIX 9:
AMA STATEMENT ON WITHHOLDING
OR WITHDRAWING LIFE-PROLONGING
MEDICAL TREATMENT

The social commitment of the physician is to sustain life and relieve suffering. Where the performance of one duty conflicts with the other, the choice of the patient, or his family or legal representative if the patient is incompetent to act in his own behalf, should prevail. In the absence of the patient's choice or an authorized proxy, the physician must act in the best interest of the patient.

For humane reasons, with informed consent, a physician may do what is medically necessary to alleviate severe pain, or cease or omit treatment to permit a terminally ill patient whose death is imminent to die. However, he should not intentionally cause death. In deciding whether the administration of potentially life-prolonging medical treatment is in the best interest of the patient who is incompetent to act in his own behalf, the physician should determine what the possibility is for extending life under humane and comfortable conditions and what are the prior expressed wishes of the patient and attitudes of the family or those who have responsibility for the custody of the patient.

Even if death is not imminent but a patient's coma is beyond doubt irreversible and there are adequate safeguards to confirm the accuracy of the diagnosis and with the concurrence of those who have responsibility for the care of the patient, it is not unethical to discontinue all means of life-prolonging medical treatment.

Life-prolonging medical treatment includes medication and artificially or technologically supplied respiration, nutrition or hydration. In treating a terminally ill or irreversibly comatose patient, the physician should determine whether the benefits of treatment outweigh its burdens. At all times, the dignity of the patient should be maintained.

APPENDIX 10:
DO NOT RESUSCITATE ORDER

Patient Name:

Patient Date of Birth:

DO NOT RESUSCITATE THE PERSON NAMED ABOVE. IF IN CARDIAC ARREST, THE INDIVIDUAL NAMED ABOVE IS TO RECEIVE NO CARDIOPULMONARY RESUSCITATION (CPR), NO ELECTRIC DEFIBRILLATION, NO TRACHEAL INTUBATION, AND NO VENTILATORY ASSISTANCE.

Effective Date:

Physician's Signature:

Print Physician's Name:

CONSENT

I understand that this document is a Do Not Resuscitate Order. I further understand that, in the event of suffering cardiac arrest, I am refusing cardiopulmonary resuscitation in situations where death may be imminent. I make this request knowingly and I am aware of the alternatives. I expressly release, on behalf of myself and my family, all persons who shall in the future attend to my medical care of any and all liability whatsoever for acting in accordance with this request.

Furthermore, I direct that these guidelines be enforced even though I may develop a diminished mental capacity in the future. I am aware that I may revoke these instructions at any time by:

(1) the physical destruction or verbal rescinding of this order by the physician who signed it; or

(2) by the physical destruction or verbal rescinding of this order by the person who gave written informed consent to the order, including myself or my legally authorized guardian, agent, or surrogate decision maker.

[Authorized signature of patient or patient's health care agent, surrogate decision maker or legal guardian]

APPENDIX 11:
RELEASE FROM LIABILITY FOR DISCONTINUING LIFE SUSTAINING TREATMENT

[I/We], the undersigned, [am/are] the [guardian/family/health care agent] of [name of patient]. [His or her] attending physician [name of physician] has advised that [patient] has suffered severe and irreversible brain injury that precludes any cognitive, meaningful or functional future existence. [Note: Or set forth a similar statement of the patient's condition].

[I/We] understand that [his or her] current survival is contingent upon [insert the procedure to be withheld or withdrawn]. It is [my/our] desire and that of the patient as expressed in [his or her] Living Will, Health Care Declaration, Durable Power of Attorney, and/or Appointment of Health Care Agent, a copy of which is attached hereto, executed on [date[s]], that all "life-sustaining procedures" as therein defined be discontinued.

By [my/our] signature(s), [I/we] hereby release and agree to hold harmless [his or her] physicians and the nurses and staff of [name of facility], from any liability, claims for damages, or causes of action that might otherwise be brought as a result of the death that likely will occur subsequent to the discontinuance of the above-described life-sustaining procedures.

SIGNATURE LINE/ADDRESS/DATE – RELEASOR

RELATIONSHIP TO PATIENT:

[specify relationship - guardian/next of kin/health care agent]

SIGNATURE LINE/ADDRESS/DATE – WITNESS #1

SIGNATURE LINE/ADDRESS/DATE – WITNESS #2

NOTARIAL ACKNOWLEDGMENT

BEFORE ME, the undersigned authority, on this day personally appeared [insert name of releasor], and [names of two witnesses], known to me to be the releasor and witnesses whose names are subscribed to the foregoing instrument in their respective capacities, and, all of said persons being by me duly sworn, [name of releasor] declared to me and to the said witnesses in my presence that said instrument is a release of liability, and that (he/she) had willingly and voluntarily made and executed it as (his/her) free act and deed for the purposes therein expressed.

SUBSCRIBED AND SWORN TO BEFORE ME by the releasor, [insert name] and by the witnesses [insert names] this _____ day of _____ _____, 20_____.

SIGNATURE LINE AND STAMP - NOTARY

APPENDIX 12:
LIVING WILL

DECLARATION made this_____day of,_____20____.

I, [Name of Declarant], residing at [Address], being of sound mind, willfully and voluntarily make known my desire that my life shall not be artificially prolonged under the circumstances set forth below, and do hereby declare:

MEDICAL CONDITION

1. If at any time I should have a terminal or incurable condition caused by injury, disease, or illness, certified to be terminal or incurable by at least two physicians, which within reasonable medical judgment would cause my death, and where the application of life-sustaining procedures would serve only to artificially prolong the moment of my death, I direct that such procedures be withheld or withdrawn, and that I be permitted to die with dignity.

2. If at any time I experience irreversible brain injury, or a disease, illness, or condition that results in my being in a permanent, irreversible vegetative or comatose state, and such injury, disease, illness, or condition would preclude any cognitive, meaningful, or functional future existence, I direct my physicians and any other attending nursing or health care personnel to allow me to die with dignity, even if that requires the withdrawal or withholding of nutrition or hydration and my death will follow such withdrawal or withholding.

LIFE-SUSTAINING PROCEDURES

It is my expressed intent that the term "life-sustaining procedures" shall include not only medical or surgical procedures or interventions that utilize mechanical or other artificial means to sustain, restore, or supplant a vital function, but also shall include the placement, withdrawal, withholding, or maintenance of nasogastric tubes, gastrostomy, intravenous lines, or any other artificial, surgical, or invasive means for nutritional support and/or hydration.

"Life-sustaining procedures" shall not be interpreted to include the administration of medication or the performance of any medical procedure deemed necessary to provide routine care and comfort or alleviate pain.

RIGHT TO REFUSE TREATMENT

It is my intent and expressed desire that this Declaration shall be honored by my family, physicians, nurses, and any other attending health care personnel as the final expression of my constitutional and legal right to refuse medical or surgical treatment and to accept the consequences of such refusal. Any ambiguities, questions, or uncertainties that might arise in the reading, interpretation, or implementation of this Declaration shall be resolved in a manner to give complete expression to my legal right to refuse treatment and shall be construed as clear and convincing evidence of my intentions and desires.

REVOCATION OF PREVIOUSLY EXECUTED DOCUMENTS

I understand the full importance of this Declaration and I am emotionally and mentally competent to make this Declaration, and by my execution, I hereby revoke any previously executed health care declaration.

COPIES AND DISTRIBUTION

The original of this document is kept at [Address]. I have made (xx#) copies of this document. Numbered and signed copies have been provided to the following individuals or institutions: [List names, addresses and phone numbers of individuals and institutions].

Signed in the presence of the witnesses who have signed below this _____ day of _____, 20____.

SIGNATURE LINE – DECLARANT

STATEMENT OF WITNESSES

I state this ___day of_____, 20____, under penalty of perjury, that the Declarant has identified himself/herself to me and that the Declarant signed or acknowledged this health care declaration in my presence.

I believe the Declarant to be of sound mind, and the Declarant has affirmed his/her awareness of the nature of this document and is signing it voluntarily and free from duress. The Declarant requested that I serve as a witness to his/her execution of this document.

I declare that I am not related to the Declarant by blood, marriage, or adoption and that to the best of my knowledge I am not entitled to any part of the estate of the Declarant on the death of the principal under a will or by operation of law.

I am not a provider of health or residential care, an employee of a provider of health or residential care, the operator of a community care facility, or an employee of an operator of a health care facility.

I declare that I have no claim against any portion of the estate of the Declarant upon his/her death, or any personal financial responsibility for the payment of Declarant's medical bills or any other of Declarant's obligations.

SIGNATURE LINE/ADDRESS/DATE – WITNESS #1

SIGNATURE LINE/ADDRESS/DATE – WITNESS #2

SIGNATURE LINE/ADDRESS/DATE – WITNESS #3

NOTARIAL ACKNOWLEDGMENT

BEFORE ME, the undersigned authority, on this day personally appeared [insert name of declarant], and [names of three witnesses], known to me to be the declarant and witnesses whose names are subscribed to the foregoing instrument in their respective capacities, and, all of said persons being by me duly sworn, [name of declarant] declared to me and to the said witnesses in my presence that said instrument is (his/her) Living Will, and that (he/she) had willingly and voluntarily made and executed it as (his/her) free act and deed for the purposes therein expressed.

SUBSCRIBED AND SWORN TO BEFORE ME by the declarant, [insert name] and by the witnesses [insert names] this _____ day of _____ _____, 20_____.

SIGNATURE LINE AND STAMP - NOTARY PUBLIC

APPENDIX 13:
DURABLE POWER OF ATTORNEY
FOR HEALTH CARE

APPOINTMENT made this day of, 20_____.

I, [insert declarant's name and address], being of sound mind, willfully and voluntarily appoint [insert health care agent's name/address/ telephone number], as my Health Care Agent (hereinafter "Agent") with a Durable Power of Attorney to make any and all health care decisions for me, except to the extent stated otherwise in this document.

EFFECTIVE DATE

This Durable Power of Attorney and Appointment of Health Care Agent shall take effect at such time as I become comatose, incapacitated, or otherwise mentally or physically incapable of giving directions or consent regarding the use of life-sustaining procedures or any other health care measures.

"Health care" in this context means any treatment, service, or procedure utilized to maintain, diagnose, or treat any physical or mental condition.

DETERMINATION OF MEDICAL CONDITION

A determination of incapacity shall be certified by my attending physician and by a second physician who is neither employed by the facility where I am a patient nor associated in practice with my attending physician and who shall be appointed to independently assess and evaluate my capacity by the appropriate administrator of the facility where I am a patient.

AUTHORITY OF HEALTH CARE AGENT

My Agent is authorized, in consultation with my attending physician, to direct the withdrawal or withholding of any life-sustaining procedures, as defined herein, as he/she solely in the exercise of his/her judgment shall determine are appropriate to give comply with my wishes and desires.

In addition, my Agent by acceptance of this Appointment agrees and is hereby directed to use his/her best efforts to make those decisions that I would make in the exercise of my right to refuse treatment and not those that he/she or others might believe to be in my best interests.

APPOINTMENT OF ALTERNATE AGENTS

If the person designated as my Agent is unable or unwilling to accept this Appointment, I designate the following persons to serve as my Agent to make health care decisions for me as authorized by this document. They shall serve in the following order:

1. First Alternate Agent: [Name, Address and Telephone No.]

2. Second Alternate Agent: [Name, Address and Telephone No.].

DURATION

[Option 1] I understand that this Power of Attorney exists indefinitely unless I define a shorter time herein or execute a revocation. If I am incapacitated at such time as this Power of Attorney expires (if applicable), the authority I have granted my Agent shall continue until such time as I am capable of giving directions regarding my health care.

[Option 2] This power of attorney ends on the following date: [insert termination date].

COPIES AND DISTRIBUTION

The original of this document is kept at [insert address where original document is kept]. I have made [#] copies of this document. Numbered and signed copies have been provided to the following individuals or institutions: [List names, addresses and phone numbers of individuals and/or institutions holding copies of the document].

Signed in the presence of the witnesses who have signed below this _____ day of _____, 20____.

NAME/ADDRESS/SIGNATURE LINE – DECLARANT

STATEMENT OF WITNESSES

I state this ___day of, 20___, under penalty of perjury, that the Declarant has identified himself/herself to me and that the Declarant signed or acknowledged this Health Care Declaration in my presence.

I believe the Declarant to be of sound mind, and the Declarant has affirmed his/her awareness of the nature of this document and is signing it voluntarily and free from duress. The Declarant requested that I serve as a witness to his/her execution of this document.

I declare that I am not related to the Declarant by blood, marriage, or adoption and that to the best of my knowledge I am not entitled to any part of the estate of the Declarant on the death of the principal under a will or by operation of law.

I am not a provider of health or residential care, an employee of a provider of health or residential care, the operator of a community care facility, or an employee of an operator of a health care facility.

I declare that I have no claim against any portion of the estate of the Declarant upon his/her death, nor any personal financial responsibility for the payment of Declarant's medical bills or any other of Declarant's obligations.

SIGNATURE LINE/ADDRESS/DATE – WITNESS #1

SIGNATURE LINE/ADDRESS/DATE – WITNESS #2

SIGNATURE LINE/ADDRESS/DATE – WITNESS #3

ACCEPTANCE BY HEALTH CARE AGENTS

HEALTH CARE AGENT (First Choice)

I, [insert name of health care agent], am willing to serve and accept the appointment as the health care agent for [insert name of declarant] as described in this document.

SIGNATURE LINE/ADDRESS/DATE – HEALTH CARE AGENT

HEALTH CARE AGENT (First Alternate)

I, [insert name of first alternate health care agent], am willing to serve and accept the appointment as the health care agent for [insert name of declarant] as described in this document, if the declarant's first choice cannot serve as health care agent.

SIGNATURE LINE/ADDRESS/DATE – HEALTH CARE AGENT

HEALTH CARE AGENT (Second Alternate)

I, [insert name of second alternate health care agent], am willing to serve and accept the appointment as the health care agent for [insert name of declarant] as described in this document, if neither the declarant's first choice nor first alternate can serve as health care agent.

SIGNATURE LINE/ADDRESS/DATE – HEALTH CARE AGENT
(Second Alternate)

NOTARIAL ACKNOWLEDGMENT

BEFORE ME, the undersigned authority, on this day personally appeared [insert name of declarant], and [names of three witnesses], and [names of three health care agents] known to me to be the declarant, witnesses, and health care agents whose names are subscribed to the foregoing instrument in their respective capacities, and, all of said persons being by me duly sworn, [name of declarant] declared to me and to the said witnesses in my presence that said instrument is (his/her) Durable Power of Attorney for Health Care, and that (he/she) had willingly and voluntarily made and executed it as (his/her) free act and deed for the purposes therein expressed.

SUBSCRIBED AND SWORN TO BEFORE ME by the declarant, [insert name], by the witnesses [insert names], and by the health care agents [insert names] this _____ day of _____, 20_____.

SIGNATURE LINE AND STAMP - NOTARY PUBLIC

APPENDIX 14:
THE PATIENT SELF-DETERMINATION
ACT OF 1990 [42 U.S.C. 1395]

SUBPART E – MISCELLANEOUS

SEC. 4751. REQUIREMENTS FOR ADVANCED DIRECTIVES UNDER STATE PLANS FOR MEDICAL ASSISTANCE.

(a) **IN GENERAL**. – Section 1902 (42 U.S.C. 1396a(a)), as amended by sections 4401(a)(2), 4601(d), 4701(a), 4711(a), and 4722 of this title, is amended

(1) in subsection (a)—

(A) by striking "and" at the end of paragraph (55),

(B) by striking the period at the end of paragraph (56) and inserting "; and:, and

(C) by inserting after paragraph (56) the following new paragraphs;

"(57) provide that each hospital, nursing facility, provider of home health care or personal care services, hospice program, or health maintenance organization (as defined in section 1903(m)(1)(A)) receiving funds under the plan shall comply with the requirements of subsection (w);

"(58) provide that the State, acting through a State agency, association, or other private nonprofit entity, develop a written description of the law of State (whether statutory or as recognized by the courts of the State) concerning advance directives that would be distributed by providers or organizations under the requirements of subsection (w)."; and

(2) by adding at the end of the following new subsection:

"(w)(1) For purposes of subsection (a)(57) and sections 1903(m)(1)(A) and 1919(c)(2)(E), the requirements of this subsection is that a provider or organization (as the case may be) maintained written policies and procedures with respect to all adult individuals receiving medical care by or through the provider or organization—

"(A) to provide written information to each such individual concerning—

"(i) an individual's rights under State law (whether statutory or as recognized by the courts of the State) to make decisions concerning such medical care, including the right to accept or refuse medical or surgical treatment and the right to formulate advance directives (as defined in paragraph (3)), and

"(ii) the provider's or organization's written policies respecting the implementation of such rights;

"(B) to document in the individual's medical record whether or not the individual has executed an advance directive;

"(C) not to condition the provision of care or otherwise discriminate against an individual based on whether or not the individual has executed an advance directive;

"(D) to ensure compliance with requirements of State law (whether statutory or as recognized by the courts of the State) respecting advance directives; and

"(E) to provide (individually or with others) for education for staff and the community on issues concerning advance directives.

Subparagraph (C) shall not be construed as requiring the provision of care which conflicts with an advance directive.

"(2) The written information described in paragraph (1)(A) shall be provided to an adult individual—

"(A) in the case of a hospital, at the time of the individual's admission as an inpatient,

"(B) in the case of a nursing facility, at the time of the individual's admission as a resident,

"(C) in the case of a provider of home health care or personal care services, in advance of the individual coming under the care of the provider,

"(D) in the case of a hospice program, at the time of initial receipt of hospice care by the individual from the program, and

"(E) in the case of a health maintenance organization, at the time of enrollment of the individual with the organization.

"(3) Nothing in this section shall be construed to prohibit the application of a State law which allows for an objection on the basis of conscience for any health care provider or any agent of such provider which as a matter of conscience cannot implement an advance directive."

"(4) In this subsection, the term 'advance directive' means a written instruction, such as a living will or durable power of attorney for health care, recognized under State law (whether statutory or as recognized by the courts of the State) and relating to the provision of such care when the individual is incapacitated.

(a) CONFORMING AMENDMENTS.—

(1) Section 1903(m)(1)(A)(42 U.S.C. 1396b(m)(1)(A)) is amended—

(A) by inserting "meets the requirement of section 1902(w)" after "which" the first place it appears, and

(B) by inserting "meets the requirement of section 1902(a) and" after "which" the second place it appears.

(2) Section 1919(c)(2) of such Act (42 U.S.C. 139r(c)(2)) is amended by adding at the end the following new subparagraph:

"(E) INFORMATION RESPECTING ADVANCE DIRECTIVES.— A nursing facility must comply with the requirements of section 1902(w) (relating to maintaining written policies and procedures respecting advance directives)."

(c) EFFECTIVE DATE.—The amendments made by this section shall apply with respect to services furnished on or after the first day of the first month beginning more than 1 year after the date of the enactment of this Act.

(d) PUBLIC EDUCATION CAMPAIGN.—

(1) IN GENERAL.— The Secretary, no later than 6 months after the date of enactment of this section, shall develop and implement a national campaign to inform the public of the option to execute advance directives and of a patient's right to participate and direct health care decisions.

(2) DEVELOPMENT AND DISTIBUTION OF INFORMATION.— The Secretary shall develop or approve nationwide informational materials that would be distributed by providers under the requirements of this section, to inform the public and the medical and legal profession of each person's right to make decisions concerning medical care, including the right to accept or refuse medical or surgical treatment, and the existence of advance directives.

(3) PROVIDING ASSISTANCE TO STATES.— The Secretary shall assist appropriate State agencies, associations, or other private entities in developing the State-specific documents that would be distributed by providers under the requirements of this section. The Secretary shall further assist appropriate State agencies, associations, or other private entities in ensuring that providers are provided a copy of the documents that are to be distributed under the requirements of the section.

(4) DUTIES OF SECRETARY.— The Secretary shall mail information to Social Security recipients, add a page to the medicare handbook with respect to the provisions of this section.

APPENDIX 15:
UNIFORM HEALTH CARE DECISIONS ACT

SECTION 1. DEFINITIONS.

(1) "Advance health-care directive" means an individual instruction or a power of attorney for health care.

(2) "Agent" means an individual designated in a power of attorney for health care to make a health-care decision for the individual granting the power.

(3) "Capacity" means an individual's ability to understand the significant benefits, risks, and alternatives to proposed health care and to make and communicate a health-care decision.

(4) "Guardian" means a judicially appointed guardian or conservator having authority to make a health-care decision for an individual.

(5) "Health care" means any care, treatment, service, or procedure to maintain, diagnose, or otherwise affect an individual's physical or mental condition.

(6) "Health-care decision" means a decision made by an individual or the individual's agent, guardian, or surrogate, regarding the individual's health care, including:

(i) selection and discharge of health-care providers and institutions;

(ii) approval or disapproval of diagnostic tests, surgical procedures, programs of medication, and orders not to resuscitate; and

(iii) directions to provide, withhold, or withdraw artificial nutrition and hydration and all other forms of health care.

(7) "Health-care institution" means an institution, facility, or agency licensed, certified, or otherwise authorized or permitted by law to provide health care in the ordinary course of business.

(8) "Health-care provider" means an individual licensed, certified, or otherwise authorized or permitted by law to provide health care in the ordinary course of business or practice of a profession.

(9) "Individual instruction" means an individual's direction concerning a health-care decision for the individual.

(10) "Person" means an individual, corporation, business trust, estate, trust, partnership, association, joint venture, government, governmental subdivision, agency, or instrumentality, or any other legal or commercial entity.

(11) "Physician" means an individual authorized to practice medicine [or osteopathy] under [appropriate statute].

(12) "Power of attorney for health care" means the designation of an agent to make health-care decisions for the individual granting the power.

(13) "Primary physician" means a physician designated by an individual or the individual's agent, guardian, or surrogate, to have primary responsibility for the individual's health care or, in the absence of a designation or if the designated physician is not reasonably available, a physician who undertakes the responsibility.

(14) "Reasonably available" means readily able to be contacted without undue effort and willing and able to act in a timely manner considering the urgency of the patient's health-care needs.

(15) "State" means a State of the United States, the District of Columbia, the Commonwealth of Puerto Rico, or a territory or insular possession subject to the jurisdiction of the United States.

(16) "Supervising health-care provider" means the primary physician or, if there is no primary physician or the primary physician is not reasonably available, the health-care provider who has undertaken primary responsibility for an individual's health care.

(17) "Surrogate" means an individual, other than a patient's agent or guardian, authorized under this [Act] to make a health-care decision for the patient.

SECTION 2. ADVANCE HEALTH-CARE DIRECTIVES.

(a) An adult or emancipated minor may give an individual instruction. The instruction may be oral or written. The instruction may be limited to take effect only if a specified condition arises.

(b) An adult or emancipated minor may execute a power of attorney for health care, which may authorize the agent to make any health-care decision the principal could have made while having capacity. The power must be in writing and signed by the principal. The power remains in effect notwithstanding the principal's later incapacity and may include individual instructions. Unless related to the principal by blood, marriage, or adoption, an agent may not be an owner, operator, or employee of [a residential long-term health-care institution] at which the principal is receiving care.

(c) Unless otherwise specified in a power of attorney for health care, the authority of an agent becomes effective only upon a determination that the principal lacks capacity, and ceases to be effective upon a determination that the principal has recovered capacity.

(d) Unless otherwise specified in a written advance health-care directive, a determination that an individual lacks or has recovered capacity, or that another condition exists that affects an individual instruction or the authority of an agent, must be made by the primary physician.

(e) An agent shall make a health-care decision in accordance with the principal's individual instructions, if any, and other wishes to the extent known to the agent. Otherwise, the agent shall make the decision in accordance with the agent's determination of the principal's best interest. In determining the principal's best interest, the agent shall consider the principal's personal values to the extent known to the agent.

(f) A health-care decision made by an agent for a principal is effective without judicial approval.

(g) A written advance health-care directive may include the individual's nomination of a guardian of the person.

(h) An advance health-care directive is valid for purposes of this [Act] if it complies with this [Act], regardless of when or where executed or communicated.

SECTION 3. REVOCATION OF ADVANCE HEALTH-CARE DIRECTIVE.

(a) An individual may revoke the designation of an agent only by a signed writing or by personally informing the supervising health-care provider.

(b) An individual may revoke all or part of an advance health-care directive, other than the designation of an agent, at any time and in any manner that communicates an intent to revoke.

(c) A health-care provider, agent, guardian, or surrogate who is informed of a revocation shall promptly communicate the fact of the revocation to the supervising health-care provider and to any health-care institution at which the patient is receiving care.

(d) A decree of annulment, divorce, dissolution of marriage, or legal separation revokes a previous designation of a spouse as agent unless otherwise specified in the decree or in a power of attorney for health care.

(e) An advance health-care directive that conflicts with an earlier advance health-care directive revokes the earlier directive to the extent of the conflict.

SECTION 4. OPTIONAL FORM.

The following form may, but need not, be used to create an advance health-care directive. The other sections of this [Act] govern the effect of this or any other writing used to create an advance health-care directive. An individual may complete or modify all or any part of the following form:

ADVANCE HEALTH-CARE DIRECTIVE

Explanation

You have the right to give instructions about your own health care. You also have the right to name someone else to make health-care decisions for you. This form lets you do either or both of these things. It also lets you express your wishes regarding donation of organs and the designa-tion of your primary physician. If you use this form, you may complete or modify all or any part of it. You are free to use a different form.

Part 1 of this form is a power of attorney for health care. Part 1 lets you name another individual as agent to make health-care decisions for you if you become incapable of making your own decisions or if you want someone else to make those decisions for you now even though you are still capable. You may also name an alternate agent to act for you if your first choice is not willing, able, or reasonably available to make decisions for you. Unless related to you, your agent may not be an owner, operator, or employee of [a residential long-term health-care institution] at which you are receiving care.

Unless the form you sign limits the authority of your agent, your agent may make all health-care decisions for you. This form has a place for you to limit the authority of your agent. You need not limit the authority of your agent if you wish to rely on your agent for all health-care decisions that may have to be made. If you choose not to limit the authority of your agent, your agent will have the right to:

(a) consent or refuse consent to any care, treatment, service, or procedure to maintain, diagnose, or otherwise affect a physical or mental condition;

(b) select or discharge health-care providers and institutions;

(c) approve or disapprove diagnostic tests, surgical procedures, programs of medication, and orders not to resuscitate; and

(d) direct the provision, withholding, or withdrawal of artificial nutrition and hydration and all other forms of health care.

Part 2 of this form lets you give specific instructions about any aspect of your health care. Choices are provided for you to express your wishes regarding the provision, withholding, or withdrawal of treatment to keep you alive, including the provision of artificial nutrition and hydration, as well as the provision of pain relief. Space is also provided for you to add to the choices you have made or for you to write out any additional wishes.

Part 3 of this form lets you express an intention to donate your bodily organs and tissues following your death.

Part 4 of this form lets you designate a physician to have primary responsibility for your health care.

After completing this form, sign and date the form at the end. It is recommended but not required that you request two other individuals to sign as witnesses. Give a copy of the signed and completed form to your physician, to any other health-care providers you may have, to any health-care institution at which you are receiving care, and to any health-care agents you have named. You should talk to the person you have named as agent to make sure that he or she understands your wishes and is willing to take the responsibility.

You have the right to revoke this advance health-care directive or replace this form at any time.

PART 1

POWER OF ATTORNEY FOR HEALTH CARE

(1) DESIGNATION OF AGENT: I designate the following individual as my agent to make health-care decisions for me:

[NAME/ADDRESS/PHONE OF INDIVIDUAL CHOSEN AS AGENT]

OPTIONAL: If I revoke my agent's authority or if my agent is not willing, able, or reasonably available to make a health-care decision for me, I designate as my first alternate agent:

[NAME/ADDRESS/PHONE OF INDIVIDUAL FIRST ALTERNATE AGENT]

OPTIONAL: If I revoke the authority of my agent and first alternate agent or if neither is willing, able, or reasonably available to make a health-care decision for me, I designate as my second alternate agent:

[NAME/ADDRESS/PHONE OF INDIVIDUAL SECOND ALTERNATE AGENT]

(2) AGENT'S AUTHORITY: My agent is authorized to make all health-care decisions for me, including decisions to provide, withhold, or withdraw artificial nutrition and hydration and all other forms of health care to keep me alive, except as I state here:

[LIST EXCEPTIONS]

(3) WHEN AGENT'S AUTHORITY BECOMES EFFECTIVE: My agent's authority becomes effective when my primary physician determines that I am unable to make my own health-care decisions unless I mark the following box.

If I mark this box [], my agent's authority to make health-care decisions for me takes effect immediately.

(4) AGENT'S OBLIGATION: My agent shall make health-care decisions for me in accordance with this power of attorney for health care, any instructions I give in Part 2 of this form, and my other wishes to the extent known to my agent. To the extent my wishes are unknown, my agent shall make health-care decisions for me in accordance with what my agent determines to be in my best interest. In determining my best interest, my agent shall consider my personal values to the extent known to my agent.

(5) NOMINATION OF GUARDIAN: If a guardian of my person needs to be appointed for me by a court, I nominate the agent designated in this form. If that agent is not willing, able, or reasonably available to act as guardian, I nominate the alternate agents whom I have named, in the order designated.

PART 2

INSTRUCTIONS FOR HEALTH CARE

If you are satisfied to allow your agent to determine what is best for you in making end-of-life decisions, you need not fill out this part of the form. If you do fill out this part of the form, you may strike any wording you do not want.

(6) END-OF-LIFE DECISIONS: I direct that my health-care providers and others involved in my care provide, withhold, or withdraw treatment in accordance with the choice I have marked below:

[ ] (a) Choice Not To Prolong Life

I do not want my life to be prolonged if

(i) I have an incurable and irreversible condition that will result in my death within a relatively short time,

(ii) I become unconscious and, to a reasonable degree of medical certainty, I will not regain consciousness, or

(iii) the likely risks and burdens of treatment would outweigh the expected benefits, OR

[ ] (b) Choice To Prolong Life

I want my life to be prolonged as long as possible within the limits of generally accepted health-care standards.

(7) ARTIFICIAL NUTRITION AND HYDRATION: Artificial nutrition and hydration must be provided, withheld, or withdrawn in accordance with the choice I have made in paragraph (6) unless I mark the following box.

If I mark this box [ ], artificial nutrition and hydration must be provided regardless of my condition and regardless of the choice I have made in paragraph (6).

(8) RELIEF FROM PAIN: Except as I state in the following space, I direct that treatment for alleviation of pain or discomfort be provided at all times, even if it hastens my death:

[LIST EXCEPTIONS]

(9) OTHER WISHES: (If you do not agree with any of the optional choices above and wish to write your own, or if you wish to add to the instructions you have given above, you may do so here.) I direct that:

[ADDITIONAL INSTRUCTIONS]

PART 3

DONATION OF ORGANS AT DEATH

(OPTIONAL)

(10) Upon my death (mark applicable box)

[ ] (a) I give any needed organs, tissues, or parts, OR

[ ] (b) I give the following organs, tissues, or parts only

(c) My gift is for the following purposes (strike any of the following you do not want)

(i) Transplant

(ii) Therapy

(iii) Research

(iv) Education

PART 4

PRIMARY PHYSICIAN

(OPTIONAL)

(11) I designate the following physician as my primary physician:

[NAME/ADDRESS/PHONE NUMBER OF PRIMARY PHYSICIAN]

OPTIONAL: If the physician I have designated above is not willing, able, or reasonably available to act as my primary physician, I designate the following physician as my primary physician:

[NAME/ADDRESS/PHONE NUMBER OF ALTERNATE PRIMARY PHYSICIAN]

(12) EFFECT OF COPY: A copy of this form has the same effect as the original.

(13) SIGNATURES: Sign and date the form here:

[SIGNATURE/DATE/ADDRESS]

OPTIONAL

SIGNATURE OF WITNESSES/DATE

SECTION 5. DECISIONS BY SURROGATE.

(a) A surrogate may make a health-care decision for a patient who is an adult or emancipated minor if the patient has been determined by the primary physician to lack capacity and no agent or guardian has been appointed or the agent or guardian is not reasonably available.

(b) An adult or emancipated minor may designate any individual to act as surrogate by personally informing the supervising health-care provider. In the absence of a designation, or if the designee is not reasonably available, any member of the following classes of the patient's family who is reasonably available, in descending order of priority, may act as surrogate:

(1) the spouse, unless legally separated;

(2) an adult child;

(3) a parent; or

(4) an adult brother or sister.

(c) If none of the individuals eligible to act as surrogate under subsection (b) is reasonably available, an adult who has exhibited special care and concern for the patient, who is familiar with the patient's personal values, and who is reasonably available may act as surrogate.

(d) A surrogate shall communicate his or her assumption of authority as promptly as practicable to the members of the patient's family specified in subsection (b) who can be readily contacted.

(e) If more than one member of a class assumes authority to act as surrogate, and they do not agree on a health-care decision and the supervising health-care provider is so informed, the supervising health-care provider shall comply with the decision of a majority of the members of that class who have communicated their views to the provider. If the class is evenly divided concerning the health-care decision and the supervising health-care provider is so informed, that class and all individuals having lower priority are disqualified from making the decision.

(f) A surrogate shall make a health-care decision in accordance with the patient's individual instructions, if any, and other wishes to the extent known to the surrogate. Otherwise, the surrogate shall make the decision in accordance with the surrogate's determination of the patient's best interest. In determining the patient's best interest, the surrogate shall consider the patient's personal values to the extent known to the surrogate.

(g) A health-care decision made by a surrogate for a patient is effective without judicial approval.

(h) An individual at any time may disqualify another, including a member of the individual's family, from acting as the individual's surrogate by a signed writing or by personally informing the supervising health-care provider of the disqualification.

(i) Unless related to the patient by blood, marriage, or adoption, a surrogate may not be an owner, operator, or employee of [a residential long-term health-care institution] at which the patient is receiving care.

(j) A supervising health-care provider may require an individual claiming the right to act as surrogate for a patient to provide a written declaration under penalty of perjury stating facts and circumstances reasonably sufficient to establish the claimed authority.

SECTION 6. DECISIONS BY GUARDIAN.

(a) A guardian shall comply with the ward's individual instructions and may not revoke the ward's advance health-care directive unless the appointing court expressly so authorizes.

(b) Absent a court order to the contrary, a health-care decision of an agent takes precedence over that of a guardian.

(c) A health-care decision made by a guardian for the ward is effective without judicial approval.

SECTION 7. OBLIGATIONS OF HEALTH-CARE PROVIDER.

(a) Before implementing a health-care decision made for a patient, a supervising health-care provider, if possible, shall promptly communicate to the patient the decision made and the identity of the person making the decision.

(b) A supervising health-care provider who knows of the existence of an advance health-care directive, a revocation of an advance health-care directive, or a designation or disqualification of a surrogate, shall promptly record its existence in the patient's health-care record and, if it is in writing, shall request a copy and if one is furnished shall arrange for its maintenance in the health-care record.

(c) A primary physician who makes or is informed of a determination that a patient lacks or has recovered capacity, or that another condition exists which affects an individual instruction or the authority of an agent, guardian, or surrogate, shall promptly record the determination in the patient's health-care record and communicate the determination to the patient, if possible, and to any person then authorized to make health-care decisions for the patient.

(d) Except as provided in subsections (e) and (f), a health-care provider or institution providing care to a patient shall:

(1) comply with an individual instruction of the patient and with a reasonable interpretation of that instruction made by a person then authorized to make health-care decisions for the patient; and

(2) comply with a health-care decision for the patient made by a person then authorized to make health-care decisions for the patient to the same extent as if the decision had been made by the patient while having capacity.

(e) A health-care provider may decline to comply with an individual instruction or health-care decision for reasons of conscience. A health-care institution may decline to comply with an individual instruction or health-care decision if the instruction or decision is contrary to a policy of the institution which is expressly based on reasons of conscience and if the policy was timely communicated to the patient or to a person then authorized to make health-care decisions for the patient.

(f) A health-care provider or institution may decline to comply with an individual instruction or health-care decision that requires medically ineffective health care or health care contrary to generally accepted health-care standards applicable to the health-care provider or institution.

(g) A health-care provider or institution that declines to comply with an individual instruction or health-care decision shall:

(1) promptly so inform the patient, if possible, and any person then authorized to make health-care decisions for the patient;

(2) provide continuing care to the patient until a transfer can be effected; and

(3) unless the patient or person then authorized to make health-care decisions for the patient refuses assistance, immediately make all reasonable efforts to assist in the transfer of the patient to another health-care provider or institution that is willing to comply with the instruction or decision.

(h) A health-care provider or institution may not require or prohibit the execution or revocation of an advance health-care directive as a condition for providing health care.

SECTION 8. HEALTH-CARE INFORMATION.

Unless otherwise specified in an advance health-care directive, a person then authorized to make health-care decisions for a patient has the same rights as the patient to request, receive, examine, copy, and consent to the disclosure of medical or any other health-care information.

SECTION 9. IMMUNITIES.

(a) A health-care provider or institution acting in good faith and in accordance with generally accepted health-care standards applicable to the health-care provider or institution is not subject to civil or criminal liability or to discipline for unprofessional conduct for:

(1) complying with a health-care decision of a person apparently having authority to make a health-care decision for a patient, including a decision to withhold or withdraw health care;

(2) declining to comply with a health-care decision of a person based on a belief that the person then lacked authority; or

(3) complying with an advance health-care directive and assuming that the directive was valid when made and has not been revoked or terminated.

(b) An individual acting as agent or surrogate under this [Act] is not subject to civil or criminal liability or to discipline for unprofessional conduct for health-care decisions made in good faith.

SECTION 10. STATUTORY DAMAGES.

(a) A health-care provider or institution that intentionally violates this [Act] is subject to liability to the aggrieved individual for damages of $[500] or actual damages resulting from the violation, whichever is greater, plus reasonable attorney's fees.

(b) A person who intentionally falsifies, forges, conceals, defaces, or obliterates an individual's advance health-care directive or a revocation of an advance health-care directive without the individual's consent, or who coerces or fraudulently induces an individual to give, revoke, or not to give an advance health-care directive, is subject to liability to that individual for damages of $[2,500] or actual damages resulting from the action, whichever is greater, plus reasonable attorney's fees.

SECTION 11. CAPACITY.

(a) This [Act] does not affect the right of an individual to make health-care decisions while having capacity to do so.

(b) An individual is presumed to have capacity to make a health-care decision, to give or revoke an advance health-care directive, and to designate or disqualify a surrogate.

SECTION 12. EFFECT OF COPY.

A copy of a written advance health-care directive, revocation of an advance health-care directive, or designation or disqualification of a surrogate has the same effect as the original.

SECTION 13. EFFECT OF [ACT].

(a) This [Act] does not create a presumption concerning the intention of an individual who has not made or who has revoked an advance health-care directive.

(b) Death resulting from the withholding or withdrawal of health care in accordance with this [Act] does not for any purpose constitute a suicide or homicide or legally impair or invalidate a policy of insurance or an annuity providing a death benefit, notwithstanding any term of the policy or annuity to the contrary.

(c) This [Act] does not authorize mercy killing, assisted suicide, euthanasia, or the provision, withholding, or withdrawal of health care, to the extent prohibited by other statutes of this State.

(d) This [Act] does not authorize or require a health-care provider or institution to provide health care contrary to generally accepted health-care standards applicable to the health-care provider or institution.

[(e) This [Act] does not authorize an agent or surrogate to consent to the admission of an individual to a mental health-care institution unless the individual's written advance health-care directive expressly so provides.]

[(f) This [Act] does not affect other statutes of this State governing treatment for mental illness of an individual involuntarily committed to a [mental health-care institution under appropriate statute].]

SECTION 14. JUDICIAL RELIEF.

On petition of a patient, the patient's agent, guardian, or surrogate, a health-care provider or institution involved with the patient's care, or an individual described in Section 5(b) or (c), the [appropriate] court may enjoin or direct a health-care decision or order other equitable relief. A proceeding under this section is governed by [here insert appropriate reference to the rules of procedure or statutory provisions governing expedited proceedings and proceedings affecting incapacitated persons].

SECTION 15. UNIFORMITY OF APPLICATION AND CONSTRUCTION.

This [Act] shall be applied and construed to effectuate its general purpose to make uniform the law with respect to the subject matter of this [Act] among States enacting it.

SECTION 16. SHORT TITLE.

This [Act] may be cited as the Uniform Health-Care Decisions Act.

SECTION 17. SEVERABILITY CLAUSE.

If any provision of this [Act] or its application to any person or circumstance is held invalid, the invalidity does not affect other provisions or applications of this [Act] which can be given effect without the invalid provision or application, and to this end the provisions of this [Act] are severable.

SECTION 18. EFFECTIVE DATE.

SECTION 19. REPEAL.

SOURCE: The National Conference of Commissioners on Uniform State Laws (NCCUSL)

APPENDIX 16:
STATE STATUTES GOVERNING ATTORNEY FEES IN MEDICAL MALPRACTICE CASES

JURISDICTION	STATUTE	APPLICABLE PROVISION
Alabama	None	None
Alaska	Alaska Statutes, § 09.60.050	Winning party in an action for damages of $1,000 or less may seek reasonable attorney fees as costs against losing party.
Arizona	Arizona Revised Statutes, § 12-568	Upon request by a party
Arkansas	None	None
California	California Bus. & Prof. Code, § 6146	Fees may not exceed 40% of first $50,000 of plaintiff recovery; 33-1/3% of next $50,000; 25% of next $500,000; 15% of any amount where the recovery exceeds $600,000.
Colorado	None	None
Connecticut	Connecticut General Statutes Annotated, § 52-251c(b)	Fees may not exceed 33-1/3% of first $300,000; 25% of next $300,000; 20% of next $300,000; 15% of next $300,000; 10% of any amount exceeding $1.2 million.
Delaware	Delaware Code Annotated, Title 18, § 6865	In a negligence action against a health care provider attorney fees are limited to 35% of first $100,000; 25% of next $100,000; 10% of balance.

JURISDICTION	STATUTE	APPLICABLE PROVISION
District of Columbia	None	None
Florida	Florida Statutes Annotated, § 766.109	Sliding scale up to damages of $2 million; 15% if settled before claim filed; 20% if settled after initial arbitration; 25% if settled within 90 days after suit filed; 30% if settled during settlement conference; 35% if settled before jury sworn; 40% if settled or paid before appeal filed; 45% if appealed. 15% where damages exceed $2 million.
Georgia	None	None
Hawaii	Hawaii Revised Statutes, Title 32, § 607-15.5	Attorney fees for plaintiff and defendant shall be limited to a "reasonable amount" as approved by the court.
Idaho	Idaho Code, § 39-4213	Contingent attorney fees shall not exceed 40% of amount recovered.
Illinois	735 ILCS 5/2-1114	33-1/3% of first $150,000; 25% of next $850,000; 20% of any recovery over $1 million.
Indiana	Indiana Code Annotated, § 16-9.5-5-1	Plaintiff's attorney fees may not exceed 15% of any award that is made from the states' patient compensation fund, which covers that portion of an award that exceeds $100,000.
Iowa	Code of Iowa, § 147.138	The court has authority to determine the reasonableness of any contingent fee arrangement between the plaintiff and the plaintiff's attorney in any personal injury or wrongful death action against specified health care providers or hospitals.
Kansas	Kansas Statutes, § 7-121b	In actions for acts or omissions of health care providers
Kentucky	None	None
Louisiana	None	None

JURISDICTION	STATUTE	APPLICABLE PROVISION
Maine	Maine Revised Statutes Annotated, Title 24, § 2961	33- 1/3% of first $100,000; 25% of next $100,000; 20% of any amount over $200,000.
Maryland	Maryland Courts & Judicial Procedure Code Annotated, § 3-2A-07	If a legal fee is in dispute, an attorney may not charge or collect compensation for services rendered in connection with a medical injury claim unless it is approved by the pretrial screening panel or by the court.
Massachusetts	Massachusetts General Laws Annotated,Chapter 231, § 60I	40% of first $150,000; 33-1/3% of next $150,000; 30% of next $200,000; 25% of any amount over $500,000.
Michigan	Michigan Court Rules, § 8.121(b)	The maximum contingency fee for a personal injury action is 33-1/3% of amount recovered.
Minnesota	None	None
Mississippi	None	None
Missouri	None	None
Montana	None	None
Nebraska	Revised Statutes of Nebraska, § 44-2834	The court shall review the attorney fees incurred by a party seeking such review and allow such compensation as the court shall deem reasonable.
Nevada	None	None
New Hampshire	New Hampshire Revised Statutes Annotated, § 508:4e	The court will review each party's attorney fees and fees for actions resulting in settlement or judgment of $200,000 or more shall be subject to court approval.
New Jersey	New Jersey Court Rules, § 1:21-7	33-1/3% of first $250,000; 25% of next $250,000; 20% of next $500,000; a reasonable fee shall be set upon all amounts recovered in excess of $500,000 upon application to the court. Where recovery is for a minor or incompetent plaintiff a fee for any amount recovered by settlement shall not exceed 25%.

JURISDICTION	STATUTE	APPLICABLE PROVISION
New Mexico	None	None
New York	New York Judicial Law § 474a	30% of first $250,000; 25% of next $250,000; 20% of next $500,000; 15% of next $250,000; 10% of amy amount which exceeds $1,250,000.
North Carolina	None	None
North Dakota	None	None
Ohio	None	None
Oklahoma	Oklahoma Statutes Annotated,Title 5, § 7	Fee may not exceed 50% of net judgment.
Oregon	Oregon Revised Statutes, § 752.150	Fee may not exceed 33-1/3% of award.
Pennsylvania	Pennsylvania Statutes Annotated, Title 40, § 1301.604	30% of first $100,000; 25% of next $100,000; 20% of balance.
Rhode Island	None	None
South Carolina	None	None
South Dakota	None	None
Tennessee	Tennessee Code Annotated,§ 29-26-120	Fee may not exceed 33-1/3% of award.
Texas	None	None
Utah	Utah Code Annotated, § 78-14-7.5	Fee may not exceed 33-1/3% of award.
Vermont	None	None
Virginia	None	None
Washington	Washington Revised Code Annotated, § 7.70.070	The court shall determine the reasonableness of each party's attorney fees.
West Virginia	None	None
Wisconsin	Wisconsin Statutes Annotated, § 655.013	33-1/3% of first $1 million or 25% of first $1 million if liability is stipulated within 180 days of filing complaint and not later than 60 days before the first day of trial; 20% of any amount in excess of $1 million.

JURISDICTION	STATUTE	APPLICABLE PROVISION
Wyoming	Wyoming Court Rules Governing Contingency Fees, Rule 6	The court shall rule on the reasonableness of contingent fee arrangements upon request of plaintiff.

Source: Compendium of Selected State Laws Governing Medical Injury Claims, U.S. Department of Health and Human Services.

APPENDIX 17:
STATE STATUTES OF LIMITATIONS IN MEDICAL MALPRACTICE CASES

JURISDICTION	STATUTE	APPLICABLE PROVISION
Alabama	Code of Alabama, §6-5-482	Within 2 years from date of injury unless injury not discovered or reasonably discoverable then suit must be brought within 6 months after discovery or when reasonably discoverable; no suit may be brought more than 4 years after date of injury; minors under 4 years must bring suit by 8th birthday if statute would have otherwise expired by that time.
Alaska	Alaska Statutes, § 09.10.070	Within 2 years from date claimant discovers, or reasonably should have discovered, the existence of all elements essential to the cause of action; tolled by disability.
Arizona	Arizona Revised Statutes, § 12-542	Within 2 years from date of injury
Arkansas	Arkansas Statutes Annotated, § 16-114-203	Within 2 years from date of accrual of cause of action; accrual of cause of action shall be date of wrongful act complained of and no other time; if latent condition due to foreign object then 1 year from discovery or reasonable discoverability; a minor aged 9 or younger with a claim as a result of obstetrical care shall have until 2 years after ninth birthday; adjudicated incompetent must bring suit within 1 year of removal of disability. California

JURISDICTION	STATUTE	APPLICABLE PROVISION
Colorado	Colorado Revised Statutes, § 13-80-102.5	Within 2 years from date of accrual but in no event more than 3 years from act; if concealment or foreign object then 2 years from discovery; if minor under 8 and less than 6 at time of injury must bring claim by age of 8.
Connecticut	Connecticut General Statutes Annotated, § 52-584	Within 2 years from injury or discovery of injury or reasonable discoverability but not more than 3 years after act or omission.
Delaware	Delaware Code Annotated, Title 18, § 6856	Within 2 years from injury or 3 years from date of injury if not discoverable; minor is same as adult or must sue by 6th birthday.
District of Columbia	DCS §12-301; 302	Within 3 years from accrual of cause of action for negligence; 1 year for battery; disability tolls statute.
Florida	Florida Statutes Annotated, § 95.11	Within 2 years from act, discovery of act, or reasonable discovery of act, but not more than 4 years; if fraud, concealment of injury or intentional misrepresentation prevented discovery within 4 year period, suit must be brought within 2 years from discovery or reasonable discovery, but in no event may suit be brought more than 7 years after act.
Georgia	Georgia Code, § 9-3-71-73	Within 2 years from injury or death but in no event longer than 5 years from act or death; 1 year after discovery if foreign object; minor under 5 years shall have 2 years from date of 5th birthday to bring action but in no event later than 10th birthday or 5 years from date of negligence; legally incompetent person must file no more than 5 years after date in which negligence, wrongful act, or omission occurred.

JURISDICTION	STATUTE	APPLICABLE PROVISION
Hawaii	Hawaii Revised Statutes, Title 32, § 657-7.3	Within 2 years from discovery or reasonable discoverability but in no event more than 6 years after act; statute is tolled during any period where the person has failed to disclose any act, error or omission upon which the action is based and which is known or reasonably knowable by that person; minors must bring action within 6 years of act or 10th birthday, whichever is longer.
Idaho	Idaho Code, § 5-219	Within 2 years from act; if foreign object or fraudulent concealment then 1 year from discovery or reasonable discovery or 2 years from act, whichever is later. Illinois,735 ILCS 5/13-212. Within 2 years from discovery or reasonable discovery of injury but in no event more than 4 years from act; statute is tolled during period plaintiff is insane, mentally ill, or imprisoned; minors must bring suit within 8 years after act but in no event after age 22.
Indiana	Indiana Code Annotated, § 16-9.5-3-1	Within 2 years from act; minor under 6 years shall have until 8th birthday to file suit; statute applies regardless of minority or other disability.
Iowa	Code of Iowa, § 614.1	Within 2 years from discovery or reasonable discoverability but in no event longer than 6 years after act unless foreign object left in body.
Kansas	Kansas Statutes, § 60-513	Within 2 years from act or reasonable discoverability but in no event more than 4 years after act.
Kentucky	Kentucky Revised Statutes, § 413.140	Within 1 year from discovery or reasonable discoverability but in no event more than 5 years after act.
Louisiana	Louisiana Revised Statutes Annotated, § 9:5628	Within 1 year from act or date of discovery but in no event more than 3 years from date of act regardless of minority or disability.
Maine	Maine Revised Statutes Annotated, Title 24, § 2902	Within 3 years after act; minors must bring action within 6 years after accrual of cause of action or within 3 years of majority, whichever occurs first.

JURISDICTION	STATUTE	APPLICABLE PROVISION
Maryland	Maryland Courts & Judicial Procedure Code Annotated, § 5-109	Within 5 years from act or 3 years from discovery, whichever is shorter; for minors statute begins to run at age 11; exceptions to statute if damages affect reproductive system or caused by foreign object.
Massachusetts	Massachusetts General Laws Annotated, Chapter 260, § 4; Chapter 231, § 60D	Within 3 years after cause of action accrues but in no event more than 7 years after act or omission unless foreign object; minors must bring action within 3 years from accrual of cause of action but if under 6 years of age statute does not begin to run until 9th birthday but in no event more than 7 years from act or omission unless foreign object.
Michigan	Michigan Comp. Laws, § 27a.5805, 5851, 5856	Within 2 years from act or 6 months from discovery or reasonable discovery; disabled plaintiff has 1 year from removal of disability except minors under 13 years have until 15th birthday; 6 years from date of injury except for reproductive injury, foreign object or fraudulent concealment.
Minnesota	Minnesota Statutes, § 541.07	Within 2 years from act.
Mississippi	Mississippi Code Annotated, § 15-1-36	Within 2 years after discovery or reasonable discoverability; minor or mentally incompetent plaintiff has within 2 years after disability ends but minor age 6 or under at time cause of action accrues has 2 years from time of 6th birthday or death, whichever occurs first.
Missouri	Missouri Revised Statutes, § 516.105	Within 2 years from act unless foreign object which is 2 years from discovery or reasonable discoverability but in no event longer than 10 years from act; minors under 10 must bring suit by 12th birthday.

JURISDICTION	STATUTE	APPLICABLE PROVISION
Montana	Montana Code Annotated, § 27-2-205	Within 3 years from act or discovery or reasonable discoverability, whichever occurs first but in no event more than 5 years from act; statute is tolled for failure of disclosure of act; minors must file within 3 years of 8th birthday or death, whichever occurs first.
Nebraska	Revised Statutes of Nebraska, § 44-2828	Within 2 years from act or 1 year from discovery but not more than 10 years after date of service which is basis for suit.
New Hampshire	New Hampshire Revised Statutes Annotated, § 508:4, 508:8	Within 3 years from act or omission or discovery or reasonable discovery; minor or incompetent must bring suit within 2 years of removal of disability.
New Jersey	New Jersey Revised Statutes, § 2A:14-2	Within 2 years after accrual of claim.
New Mexico	New Mexico Statutes Annotated, § 41-5-13	Within 3 years from date of malpractice regardless of minority or disability except minors under 6 have until 9th birthday to file suit; statute is tolled upon submission to hearing panel and shall not run until 30 days after panel's final decision.
New York	New York Civil Practice Laws and Rules, § 214-a	Within 2-1/2 years from act or last treatment where there is continuous treatment for condition giving rise to claim; if foreign object 1 year from discovery or reasonable discovery.
North Carolina	North Carolina General Statutes,§ 1-15	Cause of action shall arise at time of occurrence of last act giving rise to cause of action; where damages not readily apparent and damage is discovered or reasonably discovered 2 or more years after occurrence of last act of defendant
North Dakota	North Dakota Cent. Code, § 28-01-18; 25	Within 2 years from discovery but not more than 6 years after act unless discovery prevented by fraudulent conduct of defendant; disability except minority tolls statute for 5 years but in no case after 1 year from removal of disability; minors have 12 years to bring suit.

JURISDICTION	STATUTE	APPLICABLE PROVISION
Ohio	Ohio Revised Code Annotated, § 2305.11	Within 1 year after the accrual except if before the 1 year expires the plaintiff gives written notice then suit may be brought within 180 days of notice but in no event after 4 years from act; disability tolls statute.
Oklahoma	Oklahoma Statutes Annotated, Title 76, § 18; Title 12, § 96	Within 2 years from discovery or reasonable discoverability and medical injury suites brought more than 3 years from act shall have limited recovery; disability at time of injury tolls statute until 1 year after disability ends; minors under 12 must sue within 7 years; minors over 12 must sue within 1 year after attaining majority but in no event less than 2 years from date of injury; incompetents must sue within 7 years of injury unless adjudged incompetent then within 1 year after adjudication but in no event less than 2 years from date of injury.
Oregon	Oregon Revised Statutes, § 12.110; 160	Within 2 years from discovery or reasonable discoverability but not more than 5 years from act unless fraud; if fraud, 2 years from discovery or reasonable discovery; if minor or legal disability at time of injury then 5 years from accrual or 1 year after disability ends.
Pennsylvania	Pennsylvania Statutes Annotated, Title 42, §5524; Title 40, § 1301.605	Within 2 years; if medical injury claim filed after 4 years from act
Rhode Island	Rhode Island General Laws, § 9-1-14-1	Within 3 years from act or 3 years from discovery or reasonable discoverability; if minor or incompetent when injured then 3 years from removal of disability.
South Carolina	South Carolina Code Annotated, § 15-3-545	Within 3 years from discovery or reasonable discoverability but not more than 6 years after act; foreign object within 2 years of discovery; if minor then statute is tolled for 7 years but not more than 1 year after majority.

JURISDICTION	STATUTE	APPLICABLE PROVISION
South Dakota	South Dakota Codified Laws Annotated, § 15-2- 14.1	Within 2 years from act.
Tennessee	Tennessee Code Annotated, § 29-26-116	Within 1 year from discovery but no more than 3 years from act unless fraud; if foreign object then 1 year from discovery.
Texas	Texas Revised Statutes Annotated, Article 4590i, §10.01	Within 2 years from occurrence; minor under 12 has until 14th birthday to sue otherwise applies to all regardless of minority or disability.
Utah	Utah Code Annotated, § 78-14-4	Within 2 years from discovery or discoverability but not more than 4 years from act; if foreign object or fraud then 1 year from discovery; statute applies regardless of minority or disability.
Vermont	Vermont Statutes Annotated, Title 12, § 521	Within 3 years from act or 2 years from discovery or discoverability but no more than 7 years from act; no limitations if fraud; foreign object then 2 years from discovery.
Virginia	Virginia Code, § 8.01-243	Within 2 years from accrual or 1 year from discovery or reasonable discovery; if foreign object then 1 year from discovery or reasonable discovery unless fraud or concealment; if infant then within 5 years of accrual but in no event beyond 10 years from accrual.
Washington	Washington Revised Code Annotated, § 4.16.350	Within 3 years from act or 1 year from discovery or reasonable discoverability but no more than 8 years after act; fraud
West Virginia	West Virginia Code, § 55-7B-4	Within 2 years of injury or 2 years of discovery or reasonable discoverability

JURISDICTION	STATUTE	APPLICABLE PROVISION
Wisconsin	Wisconsin Statutes Annotated, § 893.55	Within 3 years from injury or 1 year from discovery or reasonable discoverability; if concealment or foreign object then 1 year from discovery or reasonable discoverability but in no event more than 5 years from act; minors must bring suit by age of 10 or under statute, whichever is later.
Wyoming	Wyoming Statutes, § 1-3-107	Within 2 years from act but if discovered in 2nd year plaintiff gets 6 month extension; if discovery after 2 years, plaintiff has 2 years from discovery; 1 year after removal of disability; minor must file by 8th birthday or 2 years from act.

Source: Compendium of Selected State Laws Governing Medical Injury Claims, U.S. Department of Health and Human Services.

APPENDIX 18:
STATE COLLATERAL SOURCE RULES IN MEDICAL MALPRACTICE CASES

JURISDICTION	STATUTE	APPLICABLE PROVISION
Alabama	Code of Alabama, §6-5-545	Discretionary offset; evidence of payment or future payment for medical expenses incurred by plaintiff and evidence of costs of obtaining such reimbursement or repayment is admissible.
Alaska	Alaska Statutes, § 09.55.548(b)	Mandatory offset; plaintiff may only receive damages from defendant which exceed amounts compensated by collateral sources except federal program sources which by law seek subrogation and death benefits from life insurance.
Arizona	Arizona Revised Statutes,§ 12-565	Discretionary offset; defendant may introduce evidence of collateral source of payment for economic losses. Plaintiff may introduce evidence of payment made to obtain collateral source or that recovery from defendant subject to lien or statutory subrogation.
Arkansas	None	None
California	California Civil Procedure Code, § 3333.1	Discretionary offset; defendant may introduce evidence of collateral sources; plaintiff may introduce evidence of payments made to secure collateral source benefits.

JURISDICTION	STATUTE	APPLICABLE PROVISION
		No source of collateral benefits introduced pursuant to this provision shall recovery any amount from plaintiff or be subrogated to plaintiff's rights. No collateral source shall obtain reimbursement from a medical malpractice defendant.
Colorado	Colorado Revised Statutes, § 13-21-111.5	Mandatory offset; the court will reduce amount of verdict by the sum of collateral source compensation except if the plaintiff purchased insurance that is the collateral source.
Connecticut	Connecticut General Statutes Annotated, § 52-225a	Mandatory offset; the court shall reduce the award of economic damages by the amount of compensation received from collateral sources except where a right of subrogation exists. Plaintiff may submit evidence of payments made for collateral source benefits.
Delaware	Delaware Code Annotated, Title 18, § 6862	Discretionary offset; evidence of public collateral source of compensation may be introduced including any prospective changes in the marital
District of Columbia	None	None
Florida	Florida Statutes Annotated, § 768.76	Mandatory offset of damages where liability is admitted or found by trial court by the total of all collateral source payment with exception of those collateral sources for which there are subrogation rights. Reduction shall be offset by amount paid by plaintiff
Georgia	Georgia Code, § 51-12-1	Discretionary offset; evidence of compensation from all collateral sources and costs thereof admissible for consideration by trier of fact.
Hawaii	None	None

JURISDICTION	STATUTE	APPLICABLE PROVISION
Idaho	Idaho Code, § 6-1606	Mandatory offset of collateral sources except federal benefits, life insurance, and subrogation rights.
Illinois	735 ILCS 5/2-1205	Mandatory offset; award to plaintiff shall be reduced by an amount equal to the sum of 50% of lost income collateral source benefits and 100% of health insurance benefits, except if such medial or hospital expenses are directly attributable to the medical injury at issue and to the extent there are subrogation rights. The offset shall not exceed more than 50% of the award and the offset may be reduced by the amount paid by plaintiff when the preceding two years to obtain such collateral source benefits.
Indiana	Indiana Code Annotated, § 34-4-36-2	Discretionary offset; proof of plaintiff's collateral source payments are admissible except for those payments from life insurance companies, insurance benefits directly paid for by plaintiff or plaintiff's family, and payments from state or federal sources made before trial. Proof of any subrogation rights by collateral sources against plaintiff is admissible as well as proof of the cost to plaintiff of obtaining collateral source benefits.
Iowa	Code of Iowa, § 147.146	Mandatory offset; past and future economic losses shall not be awarded to the extent that such losses are replaced or indemnified by collateral source benefits except the plaintiff's or plaintiff's family assets that have covered or will cover such losses.
Kansas	Kansas Statutes, § 60-3801	In any action for personal injury or death alleging damages in excess of $150,000, evidence of collateral sources is admissible and shall be used to reduce any damage award.

JURISDICTION	STATUTE	APPLICABLE PROVISION
Kentucky	Kentucky Revised Statutes, § 411.188	Discretionary offset; evidence of collateral source benefits, except life insurance, shall be admissible as well as the value of plaintiff premiums paid by or on behalf of plaintiff to obtain benefits and any subrogation rights.
Louisiana	None	None
Maine	Maine Revised Statutes Annotated, Title 24, § 2906	Mandatory offset; the court shall reduce the amount of the economic damage award by the amount of all collateral sources of benefits that have not exercised subrogation rights within 10 days after verdict for the plaintiff. The offset may be reduced by amounts paid by the plaintiff to obtain collateral benefits in the two year period immediately preceding the injury and the portion of plaintiff's total costs to prosecute the action, including attorney fees, may be reduced by an amount equal to the percentage that the offset is of the total award.
Maryland	None	None
Massachusetts	Massachusetts General Laws Annotated, Chapter 260, § 4; Chapter 231, § 60G	Mandatory offset; the court shall reduce the award by the amount of collateral source benefits, except for gratuitous payments. The offset will be reduced by the premiums paid by plaintiff to obtain benefits for the one year period immediately preceding the accrual of such action. No entity which is the collateral source used to reduce the award may enforce a right of subrogation against the plaintiff or otherwise recover any amount against the plaintiff.
Michigan	Michigan Comp. Laws, § 600.6303	Mandatory offset; evidence that economic damages sought have been or will be paid by collateral source, except life insurance benefits or lien holder, is admissible after verdict for the plaintiff. The amount of the offset will be reduced by the amount of premiums paid by plaintiff

JURISDICTION	STATUTE	APPLICABLE PROVISION
Minnesota	Minnesota Statutes, § 548.36	Mandatory offset; the court shall reduce the award by the amounts of collateral source benefits, except those with subrogation rights or contributed by plaintiff or his family for two years preceding action, and shall reduce the amount of offset by the amount paid by plaintiff or his family to obtain benefits.
Mississippi	None	None
Missouri	Missouri Revised Statutes, § 490.715	Evidence of special damages paid by defendant prior to trial may be introduced as collateral source benefits; no other evidence admissible.
Montana	Montana Code Annotated, § 27-1-308	Mandatory offset; where total award exceeds $50,000 and plaintiff will receive full award, the court must reduce the award by the amount of collateral source benefits that do not have subrogation rights. Amounts that a plaintiff has paid for the previous five years, or will pay, for life insurance benefits, must be deducted from the offset.
Nebraska	Revised Statutes of Nebraska,§ 44-2819	Discretionary offset; evidence of nonrefundable collateral source benefits may be taken as credit, less premium payments, against the judgment, but such evidence shall not be introduced to the jury.
Nevada	Nevada Revised Statutes, § 42.020	Damages must be reduced by amount of any prior payment made by the health care provider to the injured person or claimant to meet reasonable expenses and other essential goods and services or reasonable living expenses.
New Hampshire	New Hampshire Revised Statutes Annotated, § 507-C:7	Mandatory offset of economic damages in a medical injury action from collateral sources, minus the amounts paid by plaintiff to obtain benefits.

JURISDICTION	STATUTE	APPLICABLE PROVISION
New Jersey	New Jersey Revised Statutes, § 2A:15-97	Mandatory offset; collateral source benefits not including worker's compensation or life insurance benefits, shall be admissible and deducted from award, less any premium paid by plaintiff or plaintiff's family.
New Mexico	None	None
New York	New York Civil Practice Laws and Rules, § 4545	Mandatory offset; the court shall reduce the economic award by the amount of any collateral source benefit, except those sources with liens against the plaintiff. The court shall reduce the offset by the amount of premiums paid by plaintiff for such benefits for the two-year period immediately preceding and less the amount equal to the projected future cost of maintaining the benefit.
North Carolina	None	None
North Dakota	North Dakota Cent. Code, § 32-03.2-06	Mandatory offset; economic damages will be reduced by the amount of collateral source benefits not subject to any subrogation rights against plaintiff, or collateral source benefits purchased by the plaintiff, or life insurance benefits.
Ohio	Ohio Revised Code Annotated, § 2305.27	Mandatory offset; economic damages shall be reduced by the amount of collateral source benefits except insurance proceeds paid for by plaintiff or his employer. A collateral source of indemnity shall not be subrogated to the plaintiff against the defendant.
Oklahoma	None	None

JURISDICTION	STATUTE	APPLICABLE PROVISION
Oregon	Oregon Revised Statutes, § 18.580	Discretionary offset; court may deduct from the award the total amount of collateral source benefits other than benefits plaintiff must repay, life insurance, other insurance benefits for w which plaintiff or his family paid premiums, retirement, disability and pension plan benefits, including federal social security benefits.
Pennsylvania	Pennsylvania Statutes Annotated, Title 42, §5524; Title 40,,§ 1301.602	Mandatory offset; damages shall be reduced by any public collateral source. A right of subrogation is not enforceable against any benefit or compensation awarded or against any health care provider or its liability insurer.
Rhode Island	Rhode Island General Laws,§ 9-19-34.1	The plaintiff's award shall be reduced by jury or court by the amount of collateral benefits received less the amount paid to secure such benefits. The lien of a first party payor who has paid such a benefit shall be foreclosed.
South Carolina	None	None
South Dakota	South Dakota Codified Laws Annotated, § 21-3- 12	Discretionary offset; Where special damages are alleged, such damages may be reduced by the amount of collateral source benefits covering such damages, except to the extent that such benefits have a right of subrogation, purchased by plaintiff or his family, or are payable by government programs not subject to subrogation.
Tennessee	Tennessee Code Annotated, § 29-26-119	Mandatory offset; economic damages must be reduced by the amount of collateral source benefits received, except for assets contributed by plaintiff or his family and insurance purchased privately and individually.
Texas	None	None

JURISDICTION	STATUTE	APPLICABLE PROVISION
Utah	Utah Code Annotated, § 78-14-4.5	Mandatory offset; the court shall reduce the award by the total of all amounts from collateral source benefits, except those benefits for which subrogation rights exist. The court shall reduce offset by amounts paid by or on behalf of plaintiff to obtain benefits.
Vermont	None	None
Virginia	Virginia Code, § 8.01-35	Damages for loss of income not diminished by reimbursement to plaintiff or descendent from any source and shall not be admitted into evidence.
Washington	Washington Revised Code Annotated, § 7.70.080	Discretionary offset; evidence that the plaintiff has been compensated for injury from any sources, except patient or family assets, or insurance purchased by plaintiff or his employer, is admissible.
West Virginia	None	None
Wisconsin	None	None
Wyoming	None	None

Source: Compendium of Selected State Laws Governing Medical Injury Claims, U.S. Department of Health and Human Services.

APPENDIX 19:
HIPAA-COMPLIANT AUTHORIZATION
FOR MEDICAL RECORDS

OCA Official Form No.: 960
AUTHORIZATION FOR RELEASE OF HEALTH INFORMATION PURSUANT TO HIPAA
[This form has been approved by the New York State Department of Health]

Patient Name	Date of Birth	Social Security Number
Patient Address		

I, or my authorized representative, request that health information regarding my care and treatment be released as set forth on this form:

In accordance with New York State Law and the Privacy Rule of the Health Insurance Portability and Accountability Act of 1996 (HIPAA), I understand that:

1. This authorization may include disclosure of information relating to **ALCOHOL** and **DRUG ABUSE, MENTAL HEALTH TREATMENT**, except psychotherapy notes, and **CONFIDENTIAL HIV* RELATED INFORMATION** only if I place my initials on the appropriate line in Item 9(a). In the event the health information described below includes any of these types of information, and I initial the line on the box in Item 9(a), I specifically authorize release of such information to the person(s) indicated in Item 8.

2. If I am authorizing the release of HIV-related, alcohol or drug treatment, or mental health treatment information, the recipient is prohibited from redisclosing such information without my authorization unless permitted to do so under federal or state law. I understand that I have the right to request a list of people who may receive or use my HIV-related information without authorization. If I experience discrimination because of the release or disclosure of HIV-related information, I may contact the New York State Division of Human Rights at (212) 480-2493 or the New York City Commission of Human Rights at (212) 306-7450. These agencies are responsible for protecting my rights.

3. I have the right to revoke this authorization at any time by writing to the health care provider listed below. I understand that I may revoke this authorization except to the extent that action has already been taken based on this authorization.

4. I understand that signing this authorization is voluntary. My treatment, payment, enrollment in a health plan, or eligibility for benefits will not be conditioned upon my authorization of this disclosure.

5. Information disclosed under this authorization might be redisclosed by the recipient (except as noted above in Item 2), and this redisclosure may no longer be protected by federal or state law.

6. **THIS AUTHORIZATION DOES NOT AUTHORIZE YOU TO DISCUSS MY HEALTH INFORMATION OR MEDICAL CARE WITH ANYONE OTHER THAN THE ATTORNEY OR GOVERNMENTAL AGENCY SPECIFIED IN ITEM 9 (b).**

7. Name and address of health provider or entity to release this information:	
8. Name and address of person(s) or category of person to whom this information will be sent:	

9(a). Specific information to be released:
  ❏ Medical Record from (insert date) _____ to (insert date) _____
  ❏ Entire Medical Record, including patient histories, office notes (except psychotherapy notes), test results, radiology studies, films, referrals, consults, billing records, insurance records, and records sent to you by other health care providers.
  ❏ Other: _____   Include: (*Indicate by Initialing*)
  _____   _____ **Alcohol/Drug Treatment**
                                            _____ **Mental Health Information**
Authorization to Discuss Health Information   _____ **HIV-Related Information**

  (b) ❏ By initialing here _____ I authorize _____
                     Initials   Name of individual health care provider
    to discuss my health information with my attorney, or a governmental agency, listed here:
    _____
              (Attorney/Firm Name or Governmental Agency Name)

10. Reason for release of information:
  ❏ At request of individual
  ❏ Other:
	11. Date or event on which this authorization will expire:

12. If not the patient, name of person signing form:	13. Authority to sign on behalf of patient:

All items on this form have been completed and my questions about this form have been answered. In addition, I have been provided a copy of the form.

_____   Date: _____
Signature of patient or representative authorized by law.

* **Human Immunodeficiency Virus that causes AIDS. The New York State Public Health Law protects information which reasonably could identify someone as having HIV symptoms or infection and information regarding a person's contacts.**

Instructions for the Use
of the HIPAA-compliant Authorization Form to
Release Health Information Needed for Litigation

This form is the product of a collaborative process between the New York State Office of Court Administration, representatives of the medical provider community in New York, and the bench and bar, designed to produce a standard official form that complies with the privacy requirements of the federal Health Insurance Portability and Accountability Act ("HIPAA") and its implementing regulations, to be used to authorize the release of health information needed for litigation in New York State courts. It can, however, be used more broadly than this and be used before litigation has been commenced, or whenever counsel would find it useful.

The goal was to produce a standard HIPAA-compliant official form to obviate the current disputes which often take place as to whether health information requests made in the course of litigation meet the requirements of the HIPAA Privacy Rule. It should be noted, though, that the form is optional. This form may be filled out on line and downloaded to be signed by hand, or downloaded and filled out entirely on paper.

When filing out Item 11, which requests the date or event when the authorization will expire, the person filling out the form may designate an event such as "at the conclusion of my court case" or provide a specific date amount of time, such as "3 years from this date".

If a patient seeks to authorize the release of his or her entire medical record, but only from a certain date, the first two boxes in section 9(a) should both be checked, and the relevant date inserted on the first line containing the first box.

APPENDIX 20:
NURSING HOME CHECKLIST

 Nursing Home Checklist

Name of Nursing Home:_____ Date of Visit:_____

	Yes	No	Comments
Basic Information			
The nursing home is Medicare-certified.			
The nursing home is Medicaid-certified.			
The nursing home has the level of care needed (e.g. skilled, custodial), and a bed is available.			
The nursing home has special services if needed in a separate unit (e.g. dementia, ventilator, or rehabilitation), and a bed is available.			
The nursing home is located close enough for friends and family to visit.			
Resident Appearance			
Residents are clean, appropriately dressed for the season or time of day, and well groomed.			
Nursing Home Living Spaces			
The nursing home is free from overwhelming unpleasant odors.			
The nursing home appears clean and well-kept.			
The temperature in the nursing home is comfortable for residents.			
The nursing home has good lighting.			
Noise levels in the dining room and other common areas are comfortable.			
Smoking is not allowed or may be restricted to certain areas of the nursing home.			
Furnishings are sturdy, yet comfortable and attractive.			

Nursing Home Checklist

	Yes	No	Comments
Staff			
The relationship between the staff and the residents appears to be warm, polite, and respectful.			
All staff wear name tags.			
Staff knock on the door before entering a resident's room and refer to residents by name.			
The nursing home offers a training and continuing education program for all staff.			
The nursing home does background checks on all staff.			
The guide on your tour knows the residents by name and is recognized by them.			
There is a full-time Registered Nurse (RN) in the nursing home at in the nursing home at all times, other than the Administrator or Director of Nursing.			
The same team of nurses and Certified Nursing Assistants (CNAs) work with the same resident 4 to 5 days per week.			
CNAs work with a reasonable number of residents.			
CNAs are involved in care planning meetings.			
There is a full-time social worker on staff.			
There is a licensed doctor on staff. Is he or she there daily? Can he or she be reached at all times?			
The nursing home's management team has worked together for at least one year.			

Nursing Home Checklist

	Yes	No	Comments
Residents' Rooms			
Residents may have personal belongings and/or furniture in their rooms.			
Each resident has storage space (closet and drawers) in his or her room.			
Each resident has a window in his or her bedroom.			
Residents have access to a personal telephone and television.			
Residents have a choice of roommates.			
Water pitchers can be reached by residents.			
There are policies and procedures to protect resident's possessions.			
Hallways, Stairs, Lounges, and Bathrooms			
Exits are clearly marked.			
There are quiet areas where residents can visit with friends and family.			
The nursing home has smoke detectors and sprinklers.			
All common areas, resident rooms, and doorways are designed for wheelchair use.			
There are handrails in the hallways and grab bars in the bathrooms.			
Menus and Food			
Residents have a choice of food items at each meal. (Ask if your favorite foods are served.)			
Nutritious snacks are available upon request.			
Staff help residents eat and drink at mealtimes if help is needed.			

Nursing Home Checklist

	Yes	No	Comments
Activities			
Residents, including those who are unable to leave their rooms, may choose to take part in a variety of activities.			
The nursing home has outdoor areas for resident use and staff help residents go outside.			
The nursing home has an active volunteer program.			
Safety and Care			
The nursing home has an emergency evacuation plan and holds regular fire drills.			
Residents get preventive care, like a yearly flu shot, to help keep them healthy.			
Residents may still see their personal doctors.			
The nursing home has an arrangement with a nearby hospital for emergencies.			
Care plan meetings are held at times that are convenient for residents and family members to attend whenever possible.			
The nursing home has corrected all deficiencies (failure to meet one or more Federal or State requirements) on its last state inspection report.			

Nursing Home Checklist

Additional Comments:

GLOSSARY

Accreditation—A facility gains accreditation when it meets certain quality standards.

Accrue—To occur or come into existence.

Acknowledgement—A formal declaration of one's signature before a notary public.

Act—Legislation passed by Congress.

Action at Law—A judicial proceeding whereby one party prosecutes another for a wrong done.

Actionable—Giving rise to a cause of action.

Actionable Negligence—The breach or nonperformance of a legal duty through neglect or carelessness, resulting in damage or injury to another.

Active Euthanasia—The inducement of gentle death solely by means without which life would continue naturally.

Activities of Daily Living—Activities usually performed during the course of a normal day, e.g., bathing, dressing, eating, etc.

Actual Damages—Actual damages are those damages directly referable to the breach or tortious act, and which can be readily proven to have been sustained, and for which the injured party should be compensated as a matter of right.

Ad Damnum Clause—The clause in a complaint that sets forth the amount of damages demanded.

Advance directive—A written document that expresses an individual's preferences and instructions regarding health care in the event the individual becomes incompetent or unable to communicate or loses decision-making abilities.

Adjudication—The determination of a controversy and pronouncement of judgment.

Admissible Evidence—Evidence that may be received by a trial court to assist the trier of fact, either the judge or jury, in deciding a dispute.

Admitting Physician—The doctor that admits a person to a hospital or other in-patient health facility.

Adversary—Opponent or litigant in a legal controversy or litigation.

Adversary Proceeding—A proceeding involving a real controversy contested by two opposing parties.

Affidavit—A sworn or affirmed statement made in writing and signed; if sworn, it is notarized.

Affirmative Defense—In a pleading, a matter constituting a defense.

Agency—The relationship between a principal and an agent who is employed by the principal, to perform certain acts dealing with third parties.

Agent—An individual designated in a power of attorney for health care to make a health-care decision for the individual granting the power.

Allegation—Statement of the issue that the contributing party is prepared to prove.

Allocation—The system of ensuring that organs and tissues are distributed fairly to patients who are in need.

Alzheimer's Disease—Disorder involving deterioration of mental functions resulting from changes in brain tissues.

Ambulatory Care—Health services that do not require in-patient hospital care.

Amend—As in a pleading, to make an addition to, or a subtraction from, an already existing pleading.

American Bar Association (ABA)—A national organization of lawyers and law students.

American Arbitration Association (AAA)—National organization of arbitrators from whose panel arbitrators are selected for labor and civil disputes.

American Civil Liberties Union (ACLU)—A nationwide organization dedicated to the enforcement and preservation of rights and civil liberties guaranteed by the federal and state constitutions.

Anatomical Donation—The act of giving one's organs or tissue to someone else.

Answer—In a civil proceeding, the principal pleading on the part of the defendant in response to the plaintiff's complaint.

Appeal—Resort to a higher court for the purpose of obtaining a review of a lower court decision.

Appearance—To come into court, personally or through an attorney, after being summoned.

Appellate Court—A court having jurisdiction to review the law as applied to a prior determination of the same case.

Arbitration—The reference of a dispute to an impartial person chosen by the parties to the dispute who agree in advance to abide by the arbitrator's award issued after a hearing at which both parties have an opportunity to be heard.

Arbitration Acts—Federal and state laws that provide for submission of disputes to the process of arbitration.

Arbitration Board—A panel of arbitrators appointed to hear and decide a dispute according to the rules of arbitration.

Arbitration Clause—A clause inserted in a contract providing for compulsory arbitration in case of a dispute as to the rights or liabilities under such contract.

Arbitrator—A private, disinterested person, chosen by the parties to a disputed question, for the purpose of hearing their contention, and awarding judgment to the prevailing party.

Argument—A discourse set forth for the purpose of establishing one's position in a controversy.

Artificial Nutrition and Hydration—Food, water or other fluids that are artificially administered.

Assault—A willful attempt or threat to harm another person, which causes apprehension in that person.

Assessment—The gathering of information in order to evaluate a person's health and health-care needs.

Assumption of Risk—The legal doctrine that a plaintiff may not recover for an injury to which he assents.

Attending Physician—The doctor who is the primary caregiver for a particular patient.

Attestation—The act of witnessing an instrument in writing at the request of the party making the same, and subscribing it as a witness.

Attorney In Fact—An agent or representative of another given authority to act in that person's name and place pursuant to a document called a "power of attorney."

Award—The final and binding decision of an arbitrator, made in writing and enforceable in court under state and federal statutes.

Best Interest—In the context of refusal of medical treatment or end-of-life court opinions, a standard for making health care decisions based on what others believe to be "best" for a patient by weighing the benefits and the burdens of continuing, withholding or withdrawing treatment.

Battery—The unlawful application of force to the person of another.

Bedsore—A pressure-induced skin ulceration.

Bench—The court and the judges composing the court collectively.

Beneficiary—A person who is designated to receive property upon the death of another, such as the beneficiary of a life insurance policy, who receives the proceeds upon the death of the insured.

Benefits and Burdens—A commonly used guideline for deciding whether or not to withhold or withdraw medical treatments.

Bequest—Refers to a gift of personal property contained in a will.

Best Evidence Rule—The rule of law that requires the original of a writing, recording or photograph to be produced in order to prove its authenticity.

Best Interest—In the context of refusal of medical treatment or end-of-life court opinions, a standard for making health care decisions based on what others believe to be "best" for a patient by weighing the benefits and the burdens of continuing, withholding or withdrawing treatment.

Bill of Particulars—A request by a party for an amplification of the pleading to which it relates.

Bill of Rights—The first eight amendments to the United States Constitution.

Brain Death—Occurs when a person's brain activity stops permanently after which it is impossible to return to life.

Breach of Contract—The failure, without any legal excuse, to perform any promise that forms the whole or the part of a contract.

Breach of Duty—In a general sense, any violation or omission of a legal or moral duty.

Burden of Proof—The duty of a party to substantiate an allegation or issue to convince the trier of fact as to the truth of their claim.

Capacity—The legal qualification concerning the ability of one to understand the nature and effects of one's acts. In relation to end-of-life decision-making, a patient has medical decision making capacity if he or she has the ability to understand the medical problem and the risks and benefits of the available treatment options.

Caption—The heading of a legal document which contains the name of the court, the index number assigned to the matter, and the names of the parties.

Cardiopulmonary Resuscitation (CPR)—A group of treatments used when someone's heart and/or breathing stops in an attempt to restart the heart and breathing, including mouth-to-mouth breathing, pressing on the chest to mimic the heart's function and cause blood to circulate, electric shock, and heart-stimulating drugs.

Cause of Action—The factual basis for bringing a lawsuit.

Child Abuse—Any form of cruelty to a child's physical, moral or mental well-being.

Child Protective Agency—A state agency responsible for the investigation of child abuse and neglect reports.

Child Welfare—A generic term that embraces the totality of measures necessary for a child's well being; physical, moral and mental.

Circumstantial Evidence—Indirect evidence by which a principal fact may be inferred.

Civil Action—An action maintained to protect a private, civil right as opposed to a criminal action.

Civil Court—The court designed to resolve disputes arising under the common law and civil statutes.

Civil Law—Law that applies to non-criminal actions.

Claimant—The party who brings the arbitration petition, also known as the plaintiff.

Clear and Convincing Evidence—A high measure or degree of proof that may be required legally to prove a patient's wishes.

Codicil—A document modifying an existing will which, in order to be valid, must be formally drafted and witnessed according to statutory requirements.

Coerce—To compel by pressure, threat, or force.

Compensatory Damages—Compensatory damages are those damages directly referable to a breach or tortious act, and which can be readily proven to have been sustained, and for which the injured party should be compensated as a matter of right.

Competent Adult—An adult who is alert, capable of understanding a lay description of medical procedures and able to appreciate the consequences of providing, withholding, or withdrawing medical procedures.

Complaint—In a civil proceeding, the first pleading of the plaintiff setting out the facts on which the claim for relief is based.

Compromise and Settlement—An arrangement arrived at, either in court or out of court, for settling a dispute upon what appears to the parties to be equitable terms.

Compulsory Arbitration—Arbitration that occurs when the consent of one of the parties is enforced by statutory provisions.

Conclusion of Fact—A conclusion reached by natural inference and based solely on the facts presented.

Conclusion of Law—A conclusion reached through the application of rules of law.

Conclusive Evidence—Evidence that is incontrovertible.

Conservator—The court-appointed custodian of property belonging to a person determined to be unable to properly manage his or her property.

Constitution—The fundamental principles of law, which frame a governmental system.

Constitutional Right—Refers to the individual liberties granted by the constitution of a state or the federal government.

Contingency Fee—The fee charged by an attorney, which is dependent upon a successful outcome in the case, and is often agreed to be a percentage of the party's recovery.

Contribution—Sharing of a loss or payment among two or more parties.

Contributory Negligence—The act or omission amounting to want of ordinary care on the part of the complaining party which, concurring with the defendant's negligence, is the proximate cause of his or her injury.

Co-payment—The amount the insured may have to pay each time they receive services under their health plan.

Coroner—The public official whose responsibility it is to investigate the circumstances and causes of deaths that occur within his or her jurisdiction.

Costs—A sum payable by the losing party to the successful party for his or her expenses in prosecuting or defending a case.

Counterclaims—Counterdemands made by a respondent in his or her favor against a claimant. They are not mere answers or denials of the claimant's allegation.

Court—The branch of government responsible for the resolution of disputes arising under the laws of the government.

Cross-claim—Claim litigated by co-defendants or co- plaintiffs, against each other, and not against a party on the opposing side of the litigation.

Cross-Examination—The questioning of a witness by someone other than the one who called the witness to the stand concerning matters about which the witness testified during direct examination.

Custodial Care—Nonskilled, personal care, such as assistance with activities of daily living.

Damages—In general, damages refers to monetary compensation which the law awards to one who has been injured by the actions of another, such as in the case of tortious conduct or breach of contractual obligations.

Decedent—A deceased person.

Decree—A decision or order of the court.

Defendant—In a civil proceeding, the party responding to the complaint.

Defense—Opposition to the truth or validity of the plaintiff's claims.

Dehydration—Condition whereby a person's loss of bodily fluid exceeds his or her fluid intake.

Delirium—A mix of short-term problems with focusing or shifting attention, being confused and not being aware of one's surroundings.

Dementia—The irreversible deterioration of mental faculties.

Deposition—A method of pretrial discovery that consists of a statement of a witness under oath, taken in question and answer form as it would be in court, with opportunity given to the adversary to be present and cross-examine.

Discharge Plan—A plan that describes the arrangements for any health care services a patient may need after leaving the hospital.

Discovery—Modern pretrial procedure by which one party gains information held by another party.

Do-Not-Resuscitate (DNR) Order—A physician's written order instructing health care providers not to attempt cardiopulmonary resuscitation (CPR) in case of cardiac or respiratory arrest.

Due Process Rights—All rights, which are of such fundamental importance as to require compliance with due process standards of fairness and justice.

Durable Power of Attorney for Health Care—Also known as a "health care proxy," refers to a document naming a person to make medical decisions in the event that the individual becomes unable to make those decisions on his or her own behalf.

Duress—Refers to the action of one person which compels another to do something he or she would not otherwise do.

Duty—The obligation, to which the law will give recognition and effect, to conform to a particular standard of conduct toward another.

Edema—Excessive accumulation of water in the tissues.

Elder Law—Laws regarding the rights of elderly people.

Elopement—The ability of a nursing home resident who is not capable of self-preservation to successfully leave the nursing home unsupervised and undetected and enter into a harmful situation.

Emergency Medical Services (EMS)—A group of governmental and private agencies that employ paramedics, first responders, and other ambulance crew to provide emergency care to persons outside of health care facilities.

End-Stage Organ Disease—A disease that ultimately leads to functional failure of an organ, e.g., emphysema (lungs), cardiomyopathy (heart), and polycystic kidney disease (kidneys).

End-Stage Renal Disease (ESRD)—A very serious and life-threatening kidney disease, which is treated by dialysis and kidney transplantation.

Euthanasia—The act of painlessly assisting in the death of a person suffering from terminal illness or other prolonged suffering. Literally means "good death" in Greek.

Execution—The performance of all acts necessary to render a written instrument complete, such as signing, sealing, acknowledging, and delivering the instrument.

Expert Witness—A witness who has special knowledge about a certain subject, upon which he or she will testify, which knowledge is not normally possessed by the average person.

Eyewitness—A person who can testify about a matter because of his or her own presence at the time of the event.

Fact Finder—In a judicial or administrative proceeding, the person, or group of persons, that has the responsibility of determining the acts relevant to decide a controversy.

Finding—Decisions made by the court on issues of fact or law.

Foreseeability—A concept used to limit the liability of a party for the consequences of his acts to consequences that are within the scope of a foreseeable risk.

Fraud—A false representation of a matter of fact, whether by words or by conduct, by false or misleading allegations, or by concealment of that which should have been disclosed, which deceives and is intended to deceive another, and thereby causes injury to that person.

General Damages—General damages are those damages directly referable to the breach or tortious act and which can be readily proven to have been sustained, and for which the injured party should be compensated as a matter of right.

Gerontology—The study of the elderly and the aging process.

Gross Negligence—The intentional failure to meet the required standard of care in reckless disregard of the consequences to another.

Guardian—A person who is entrusted with the management of the property and/or person of another who is incapable, due to age or incapacity, to administer their own affairs.

Guardian Ad Litem—Person appointed by a court to represent a minor or incompetent for purpose of some litigation.

Health Care—Any care, treatment, service, or procedure to maintain, diagnose, or otherwise affect an individual's physical or mental condition.

Health Care Agent—The person named in an advance directive or as permitted under state law to make health care decisions on behalf of a person who is no longer able to make medical decisions.

Health Care Decision—A decision made by an individual or the individual's agent, guardian, or surrogate, regarding the individual's health care, including: (1) selection and discharge of health-care providers and institutions; (2) approval or disapproval of diagnostic tests, surgical procedures, programs of medication, and orders not to resuscitate; and (3) directions to provide, withhold, or withdraw artificial nutrition and hydration and all other forms of health care.

Health Care Institution—An institution, facility, or agency licensed, certified, or otherwise authorized or permitted by law to provide health care in the ordinary course of business.

Health Care Provider—A person who is licensed, certified, registered, or otherwise authorized by law to administer or provide health care in the ordinary course of business or in the practice of a profession.

Health Care Proxy—Any person lawfully designated to act on behalf of an individual.

Hospice Care—A program model for delivering palliative care to individuals who are in the final stages of terminal illness.

Illegal—Against the law.

Immaterial—Evidence that is not offered to prove a material issue.

Impeach—A showing by means of evidence that the testimony of a witness was unworthy of belief. Also refers to the process of charging a public official with a wrong while still holding office.

Impleader—The process of bringing a third potentially liable party into a pending suit.

Implied Consent—Consent that is manifested by signs, actions or facts, or by inaction or silence, which raises a presumption that consent has been given.

Incapacity—A defense to breach of contract that refers to a lack of legal, physical or intellectual power to enter into a contract.

Incompetency—Lack of legal qualification or fitness to discharge a legally required duty or to handle one's own affairs; also refers to matters not admissible in evidence.

Infancy—The state of a person who is under the age of legal majority.

Informed Consent—The requirement that a patient be apprised of the nature and risks of a medical procedure before the physician can validly claim exemption from liability for battery, or from responsibility for medical complications.

Injury—Any damage done to another's person, rights, reputation or property.

Inspection Report—Written findings that support a federal or state determination that a nursing home failed to meet certain federal regulations or state requirements.

Intentional Tort—A tort or wrong perpetrated by one who intends to do that which the law has declared wrong, as contrasted with negligence in which the tortfeasor fails to exercise that degree of care in doing what is otherwise permissible.

Interrogatories—A pretrial discovery method whereby written questions are served by one party to the action upon the other, who must reply, in writing, under oath.

Intubation—Refers to "endotracheal intubation"—i.e., the insertion of a tube through the mouth or nose into the trachea to create and maintain an open airway to assist breathing.

Joint and Several—The rights and liabilities shared among a group of people individually and collectively.

Judge—The individual who presides over a court, and whose function it is to determine controversies.

Judgment—A final determination by a court of law concerning the rights of the parties to a lawsuit.

Jurisdiction—The power to hear and determine a case.

Jury—A group of individuals summoned to decide the facts in issue in a lawsuit.

Jury Trial—A trial during which the evidence is presented to a jury so that they can determine the issues of fact, and render a verdict based upon the law as it applies to their findings of fact.

Lay Witness—Any witness not testifying as an expert witness.

Legal Aid—A national organization established to provide legal services to those who are unable to afford private representation.

Legal Capacity—Referring to the legal capacity to sue, it is the requirement that a person bringing the lawsuit have a sound mind, be of lawful age, and be under no restraint or legal disability.

Legislation—Laws enacted by state or federal representatives.

Life Expectancy—The period of time that a person is statistically expected to live, based on such factors as their present age and sex.

Life Insurance—A contract between an insured and an insurer whereby the insurer promises to pay a sum of money upon the death of the insured to his or her designated beneficiary, in return for the periodic payment of money, known as a premium.

Life-Sustaining Treatment—Any medical treatment, procedure, or intervention that, in the judgment of the attending physician, when applied to the patient, would serve only to prolong the dying process where the patient has a terminal illness or injury, or would serve only to maintain the patient in a condition of permanent unconsciousness.

Living Will—A declaration that states an individual's wishes concerning the use of extraordinary life support systems.

Long Term Care—The services provided at home or in an institutionalized setting to older persons who require medical or personal care for an extended period of time.

Long-Term Care Ombudsman—An independent advocate for nursing home residents.

Malfeasance—The commission of a wrongful act.

Malnutrition—A serious health problem caused by poor nutrition.

Mechanical ventilation—Mechanical ventilation is used to support or replace the function of the lungs by use of a machine called a ventilator that forces air into the lungs.

Medicaid—A federal program, financed by federal, state and local governments, intended to provide access to health care services for the poor.

Medical Malpractice—The failure of a physician to exercise that degree of skill and learning commonly applied under all the circumstances in the community by the average prudent reputable professional in the same field.

Medicare—The program governed by the Social Security Administration to provide medical and hospital coverage to the aged or disabled.

Mental Abuse—The intentional infliction of anguish, degradation, fear, or distress through verbal or nonverbal acts.

Minor—A person who has not yet reached the age of legal competence, which is designated as 18 in most states.

Misfeasance—Improper performance of a lawful act.

Motion—An application to the court requesting an order or ruling in favor of the applicant.

Narcotics—Generic term for any drug that dulls the senses or induces sleep and which commonly becomes addictive after prolonged use.

Neglect—Referring to a nursing home resident, the failure to provide a resident with the proper care needed to avoid harm or illness.

Negligence—The failure to exercise the degree of care that a reasonable person would exercise given the same circumstances.

Negligence Per Se—Conduct, whether of action or omission, which may be declared and treated as negligence without any argument or proof as to the particular surrounding circumstances, because it is contrary to the law.

Nominal Damages—A trivial sum of money which is awarded as recognition that a legal injury was sustained, although slight.

Non Obstante Verdicto (N.O.V.)—Latin for "notwithstanding the verdict." It refers to a judgment of the court that reverses the jury's verdict, based on the judge's determination that the verdict has no basis in law or is unsupported by the facts.

Notice of Petition—Written notice of a petitioner that a hearing will be held in a court to determine the relief requested in an annexed petition.

Nursing Home—A residential facility that gives nursing care or custodial care to an ill or injured person.

Nursing Home Abuse—The infliction of physical pain or injury on a nursing home resident by a person having care or custody over the resident.

Nursing Home Negligence—The failure to exercise the requisite standard of care in connection with the treatment and supervision of a nursing home resident.

Nursing Home Reform Act of 1987—Federal law governing nursing homes which gives nursing home residents certain rights.

Oath—A sworn declaration of the truth under penalty of perjury.

Objection—The process by which it is asserted that a particular question, or piece of evidence, is improper, and it is requested that the court rule upon the objectionable matter.

Ombudsman—Under certain state laws, an individual licensed to oversee various health care issues.

Out-of-Pocket Maximum—Refers to the maximum amount an insured may have to pay in coinsurance payments for covered services under the plan each year before the plan begins paying the full amount of covered services.

Pain and Suffering—Refers to damages recoverable against a wrongdoer which include physical or mental suffering.

Palliative care—A comprehensive approach to treating serious illness that focuses on the physical, psychological, spiritual, and existential needs of the patient--sometimes called "comfort care" or "hospice type care."

Parens Patriae—Latin for "parent of his country." Refers to the role of the state as guardian of legally disabled individuals.

Party—Person having a direct interest in a legal matter, transaction or proceeding.

Peer Review Organization (PRO)—The agencies responsible for ongoing review of the inpatient hospital care provided to people who are eligible for Medicare.

Permanent Unconsciousness—A condition that, to a reasonable degree of medical certainty: (1) will last permanently, without improvement; and (2) in which cognitive thought, sensation, purposeful action, social interaction, and awareness of self and environment are absent; and (3) which condition has existed for a period of time sufficient, in accordance with applicable professional standards, to make such a diagnosis; and (4) which condition is confirmed by a physician who is qualified and experienced in making such a diagnosis.

Person—An individual, corporation, business trust, estate, trust, partnership, association, joint venture, government, governmental subdivision or agency, or any other legal or commercial entity.

Petition—A formal written request to a court, which initiates a special proceeding.

Petitioner—In a special proceeding, one who commences a formal written application, requesting some action or relief, addressed to a court for determination.

Physician—A person licensed by the state to practice medicine.

Plan of Care—Refers to the comprehensive individualized care plan for residents required under the Nursing Home Reform Act of 1987.

Plaintiff—In a civil proceeding, the one who initially brings the lawsuit.

Pleadings—Refers to plaintiff's complaint which sets forth the facts of the cause of action, and defendant's answer that sets forth the responses and defenses to the allegations contained in the complaint.

Post Mortem—Latin for "after death." Refers to the coroner's examination of a body to determine cause of death.

Power of Attorney—A legal document authorizing another to act on one's behalf.

Prima Facie Case—A case which is sufficient on its face, being supported by at least the requisite minimum of evidence, and being free from palpable defects.

Primary Physician—A physician designated by an individual or the individual's agent, guardian, or surrogate, to have primary responsibility for the individual's health care or, in the absence of a designation or if the designated physician is not reasonably available, a physician who undertakes the responsibility.

Procurement—The process of retrieving organs and/or tissue from a donor.

Proximate Cause—That which, in a natural and continuous sequence, unbroken by any efficient intervening cause, produces injury, and without which the result would not have occurred.

Punitive Damages—Compensation in excess of compensatory damages that serves as a form of punishment to the wrongdoer who has exhibited malicious and willful misconduct.

Quality Improvement Organizations—Groups of practicing doctors and other health care experts that are paid by the Federal government to check and improve the care given to Medicare patients.

Question of Fact—The fact in dispute that is the province of the trier of fact, i.e. the judge or jury, to decide.

Question of Law—The question of law that is the province of the judge to decide.

Release—A document signed by one party, releasing claims he or she may have against another party, usually as part of a settlement agreement.

Relief—The remedies afforded a complainant by the court.

Res Ipsa Loquitur—Literally, "the thing speaks for itself." Refers to an evidentiary rule which provides that negligence may be inferred from the fact that an accident occurred when such an occurrence would not ordinarily have happened. In the absence of negligence, the cause of the occurrence was within the exclusive control of the defendant, and the plaintiff was in no way at fault.

Respiratory arrest—The cessation of breathing, i.e., an event in which an individual stops breathing and if breathing is not restored, an individual's heart eventually will stop beating, resulting in cardiac arrest.

Respondent—The responding party, also known as the defendant.

Restatement of the Law—A series of volumes authored by the American Law Institute that tell what the law in a general area is, how it is changing, and what direction the authors think this change should take.

Restraints—Any method or device designed to restrict the movement of one's body.

Retainer Agreement—A contract between an attorney and the client stating the nature of the services to be rendered and the cost of the litigation.

Service of Process—The delivery of legal court documents, such as a complaint, to the defendant.

Settlement—An agreement by the parties to a dispute on a resolution of the claims, usually requiring some mutual action, such as payment of money in consideration of a release of claims.

Sexual Abuse—Nonconsensual sexual contact.

Skilled Nursing Care—A level of care that must be provided or supervised by a registered nurse.

Skilled Nursing Facility—A nursing facility with a staff and equipment able to give skilled nursing care.

Statute—A law.

Suicide—The deliberate termination of one's existence.

Summons—A mandate requiring the appearance of the defendant in an action under penalty of having judgment entered against him for failure to do so.

Surrogate—A person designated to make health care decisions for another individual if that individual is unable to make or communicate these decisions.

Survival Statute—A statute that preserves for a decedent's estate a cause of action for infliction of pain and suffering and related damages suffered up to the moment of death.

Respiratory arrest—The cessation of breathing, i.e., an event in which an individual stops breathing and if breathing is not restored, an individual's heart eventually will stop beating, resulting in cardiac arrest.

Terminal Illness—An incurable condition caused by injury, disease or illness which, regardless of the application of life-sustaining procedures would, within reasonable medical judgment, produce death and where the application of life-sustaining procedures serve only to postpone the moment of death of the patient.

Terminally Ill Patient—A patient whose death is imminent or whose condition, to a reasonable degree of medical certainty, is hopeless unless he or she is artificially supported through the use of life-sustaining procedures and which condition is confirmed by a physician who is qualified and experienced in making such a diagnosis.

Testify—The offering of a statement in a judicial proceeding, under oath and subject to the penalty of perjury.

Testimony—The sworn statement make by a witness in a judicial proceeding.

Tort—A private or civil wrong or injury, other than breach of contract, for which the court will provide a remedy in the form of an action for damages.

Tortfeasor—A wrong-doer.

Tortious Conduct—Wrongful conduct, whether of act or omission, of such a character as to subject the actor to liability under the law of torts.

Transcript—An official and certified copy of what transpired in court or at an out-of-court deposition.

Transplantation—The transfer of cells, tissues, or organs from an area of the body to another or from one organism to another.

Transplant Centers—Hospitals or medical centers that perform organ and/or tissue transplants.

Trial—The judicial procedure whereby disputes are determined based on the presentation of issues of law and fact. Issues of fact are decided by the trier of fact, either the judge or jury, and issues of law are decided by the judge.

Trial Court—The court of original jurisdiction over a particular matter.

Unconstitutional—Refers to a statute which conflicts with the United States Constitution rendering it void.

Undue Influence—Abuse of position of trust in order to induce a person to do or refrain from doing something.

Unfit—Incompetent.

Uniform Laws—Laws that have been approved by the Commissioners on Uniform State Laws, and which are proposed to all state legislatures for consideration and adoption.

Venue—The proper place for trial of a lawsuit.

Verdict—The definitive answer given by the jury to the court concerning the matters of fact committed to the jury for their deliberation and determination.

Verification—The confirmation of the authenticity of a document, such as an affidavit.

Vicarious Liability—In tort law, refers to the liability assessed against one party due to the actions of another party.

Voluntary Arbitration—Arbitration that occurs by mutual and free consent of the parties.

Waiver—An intentional and voluntary surrender of a right.

Ward—A person over whom a guardian is appointed to manage his or her affairs.

Will—A legal document which a person executes setting forth their wishes as to the distribution of their property upon death.

Withholding or Withdrawing Treatment—Forgoing life-sustaining measures or discontinuing them after they have been used for a certain period of time.

Witness—One who testifies to what he has seen, heard, or otherwise observed.

Wrongful Death Action—An action brought to recover damages for the death of a person caused by the wrongful act or neglect of another.

Wrongful Death Statute—A statute that creates a cause of action for any wrongful act, neglect, or default that causes death.

Wrongful Life—In tort law, refers to the birth of a child that should not have occurred for some reason, e.g., the negligent performance of a sterilization procedure.

X—Refers to the mark that may be used to denote one's signature when the signer is unable to write his or her name.

BIBLIOGRAPHY AND ADDITIONAL RESOURCES

American Board of Medical Specialties (Date Visited: October 2007) http://www.abms.org/

American Medical Association (Date Visited: October 2007) http://www.ama-assn.org/

Association for Responsible Medicine (Date Visited: October 2006) http://www.a-r-m.org/

Black's Law Dictionary, Fifth Edition. St. Paul, MN: West Publishing Company, 1979.

Center for Medicare Advocacy (Date Visited: October 2007) http://www.medicareadvocacy.org/

Centers for Disease Control (Date Visited: October 2007) http://www.cdc.gov/

Centers for Medicare & Medicaid Services (Date Visited: October 2007) http://www.medicare.gov/

Federation of State Medical Boards (Date Visited: October 2007) http://www.fsmb.org/

Health Care Choices (Date Visited: October 2007) http://www.healthcarechoices.org/

The Joint Commission (Date Visited: October 2007) http://www.jcaho.org/

Medical Review Foundation, Inc. (Date Visited: October 2007) http://www.malpracticeexperts.com/

Medicare Rights Center (Date Visited: October 2007) http://www.medicarerights.org/

National Academy of Elder Law Attorneys (Date Visited: October 2007) http://www.naela.org/

National Health Law Program (Date Visited: October 2007) http://www.healthlaw.org/

National Institute on Aging (Date Visited: October 2007) http://www.nia.nih.gov/

National Senior Citizens Law Center (Date Visited: October 2007) http://www.nsclc.org/

Nursing Home Info (Date Visited: October 2007) http://www.nursinghomeinfo.com/

U.S. Department of Health and Human Services (Date Visited: October 2007) http://www.hhs.gov/

U.S. Food and Drug Administration (Date Visited: October 2007) http://www.fda.gov/